VIETNAM'S FINAL AIR CAMPAIGN

OPERATION LINEBACKER I & II
MAY–DECEMBER 1972

STEPHEN EMERSON

Pen & Sword
MILITARY

First published in Great Britain in 2019 by
PEN AND SWORD MILITARY
an imprint of
Pen and Sword Books Ltd
47 Church Street
Barnsley
South Yorkshire S70 2AS

ISBN 978 1 52672 845 6

Maps & diagrams by George Anderson
Typeset by Aura Technology and Software Services, India
Printed and bound by CPI Group (UK) Ltd, Croydon CR0 4YY

Pen & Sword Books Ltd incorporates the imprints of Pen & Sword
Archaeology, Atlas, Aviation, Battleground, Discovery, Family History, History, Maritime, Military,
Naval, Politics, Railways, Select, Social History, Transport, True Crime, Claymore Press, Frontline
Books, Leo Cooper, Praetorian Press, Remember When, Seaforth Publishing and Wharncliffe.

For a complete list of Pen and Sword titles please contact
Pen and Sword Books Limited
47 Church Street, Barnsley, South Yorkshire, S70 2AS, England
email: enquiries@pen-and-sword.co.uk
website: www.pen-and-sword.co.uk

Stephen Emerson was born in San Diego, California into a U.S. Navy family; his father was a career naval aviator and his mother a former Navy nurse. Steve and his siblings grew up on various Navy bases during the Vietnam War. His father served two combat tours as an attack pilot in Vietnam flying the A-4 Skyhawk as part of Operation Rolling Thunder while flying off the USS *Midway* in 1965 with VA-22 and later as commanding officer of VA-146 flying the A-7 Corsair II while embarked on the USS *Enterprise* in 1969. Steve holds a Ph.D. in International Relations/Comparative Politics from the University of Florida and currently resides in Orlando, Florida. His most recent book, *Air War Over North Vietnam: Operation Rolling Thunder, 1965–1968*, examines initial American efforts to use air power as a tool of coercive diplomacy.

CONTENTS

List of Maps & Charts

GLOSSARY

AGM-45	Shrike air-to-ground homing missile with 150-pound warhead
AGM-62	Walleye air-to-ground guided missile with 825-pound warhead
AGM-78	Standard ARM (Anti-Radiation Missile) with 215-pound warhead
AIM-7	Sparrow air-to-air radar homing missile
AIM-9	Sidewinder air-to-air heat seeking missile
ALQ pods	externally-mounted electronic warfare jamming pods
alpha strike	large-scale airstrike against a fixed target
Arc Light	B-52 carpet bombing mission
armed recce	roaming air reconnaissance patrol seeking out targets of opportunity
Atoll missile	Soviet air-to-air missile used by MiG-21s that was a Soviet copy of the U.S. AIM-9 Sidewinder missile
Buff	Air Force nickname for the B-52 Stratofortress; Big Ugly Fat Fellow/F*cker
CAG	Carrier Air Group commander; senior officer in charge of all squadrons aboard an aircraft carrier. Term was retained even after Navy changed from Carrier Air Groups to Carrier Air Wings.
chaff	thin strips of aluminum or coated fiberglass disbursed by aircraft to confuse enemy radar and weapons guidance systems
CVW	Carrier Air Wing; composed of all squadrons assigned to an aircraft carrier. Every aircraft carrier had its own unique numbered air wing, i.e., CVW-2, under command of a CAG.
DMZ	demilitarized zone dividing North and South Vietnam
ECM	electronic countermeasures
EOGB	electro-optically guided bomb, also called television-guided bombs
Iron Hand	SAM suppression mission
LGB	laser-guided bomb
MACV	Military Assistance Command Vietnam; established 1962
MK-20	Rockeye cluster bomb
MK-36 DST	Modified MK-82 500-pound bomb for use as an aerial delivered magnetic-triggered Destructor mine
MK-52	Specially designed 1,000-pound-class air-laid sea mine with acoustic, magnetic, and pressure trigger settings
MK-81	250-pound bomb
MK-82	500-pound bomb
MK-82 Snakeye	500-pound bomb equipped with stabilizing fins for low level bombing
MK-83	1,000-pound bomb

MK-84	2,000-pound bomb
M117	Air Force 750-pound bomb
M118	Air Force 3,000-pound bomb
Operation Barrel Roll	Northern Laos operating area; part of U.S. interdiction effort
Operation Commando Hunt	Southern Laos interdiction effort against the Ho Chi Minh Trail
Operation Igloo White	Airborne sowing of more than 20,000 seismic and acoustic sensors along the Ho Chi Minh Trail to detect enemy movements
Operation Menu	secret bombing of Cambodia in 1970
Paveway	Precision avionics vectoring system that attached to normal 2,000 or 3,000-pound bomb to become a laser-guide munition
POL	petroleum, oil, and lubricants
Red Crown	Call sign for the Navy's Positive Identification Radar Advisory Zone ship in the Gulf of Tonkin tasked with monitoring and reporting enemy air movements in real time.
Route Package	Also called Route Pack. A geographic operating area of North Vietnam; numbered I to V plus VI A and VI B.
SA-2	Soviet-made Guideline surface-to-air missile
SA-7	Soviet-made Strela handheld, portable surface-to-air missile
SAM	surface-to-air missile
Shrike	air-to-ground homing missile with 150-pound warhead; officially AGM-45
SW	strategic wing (Air Force)
TEWS	tactical electronic warfare squadron (Air Force)
TF-77	Task Force 77; naval carrier task force component of Seventh Fleet
TFS	tactical fighter squadron (Air Force)
TFW	tactical fighter wing (Air Force)
TRW	tactical reconnaissance wing (Air Force)
VA	attack squadron (Navy)
VF	fighter squadron (Navy)
VNAF	Republic of Vietnam Air Force (South Vietnam)
VPAF	Vietnamese People's Air Force (North Vietnam)
Walleye	air-to-ground guided missile with 825-pound warhead; officially AGM-62
Wild Weasel	F-105G and F-4C air defense suppression and radar jamming aircraft (Air Force)
Yankee Station	Codename for Navy carrier operating point in the Gulf of Tonkin that supported air operations in North Vietnam, Laos, and South Vietnam.

ACKNOWLEDGEMENTS

Special thanks to the National Museum of the Air Force in Dayton, Ohio and especially to archivist Brett Stolle for his invaluable assistance in helping me research the museum's data and photo collections.

Special thanks to the Naval Aviation Museum in Pensacola, Florida and the volunteer staff of the Emil Buehler Library for their assistance in locating files and photos.

I am grateful to the Department of the Air Force and the Department of the Navy, including the Air Force Historical Research Agency at Maxwell AFB, Alabama and the Naval History and Heritage Command in Washington, DC, for their commitment to enhancing public access to official photographic and documentary materials concerning the Vietnam War.

I would also like to extend my appreciation to those Vietnam aviators I consulted for assistance with questions about technical and operational details, notably those "River Rats" Stan Goldstein and Howard Plunkett of the Red River Valley Fighter Pilots Association.

Deep appreciation to all the writers and researchers before me, who have contributed to the large—and growing—body of literature on the air war in Vietnam; much of which I have consulted for this book. Special recognition is given to Chris Hobson's *Vietnam Air Losses*, John Morrocco's *Rain of Fire*, Elizabeth Hartsook and Stuart Slade's *Air War Vietnam Plans and Operations*, Marshall Michel's *The 11 Days of Christmas*, and Karl Eschmann's *Linebacker* (perhaps the most definitive, detailed account of Linebacker II), which are indispensable reference works for anyone delving into the final years of the air war in Vietnam. Lien-Hang Nguyen's book, *Hanoi's War*, provides an interesting counterpoint from the North Vietnamese perspective and is well worth reading.

Finally, to all the men who flew in or supported Operation Linebacker I & II in 1972. You had a difficult job to do at a trying time in American history, but you did it with the highest degree of dedication and professionalism.

1. SEARCHING FOR PEACE WITH HONOR

In 1972 the U.S. military involvement in the Vietnam was coming to an end. Since coming to office in January 1969, President Richard Nixon and his administration had repeatedly pledged to bring American boys home and end the war. A war that was costly not only in terms of blood and treasure, but one that had torn apart the political and social fabric of the country. Getting out of Vietnam would be the first step in trying to heal the wounds of a deeply divided nation. It was only a question of time and circumstance.

From their peak of 543,000 in April 1969, U.S. troop levels had fallen precipitously to 156,800 by January 1972 and were on track to be less than half that number by the spring. Moreover, the American withdrawal continued despite the lack of significant progress in ongoing peace talks with U.S. forces largely assuming a supporting, training, and advisory role as the policy of Vietnamization of the war took hold. The burden of fighting was being passed exclusively to the well-equipped and -supplied, but often poorly led, Army of the Republic of Vietnam (ARVN). Likewise, American air assets in Southeast Asia were being reduced, although U.S. air capability in theater still remained substantial. As the drawdown continued and peace talks dragged on in Paris throughout 1972, it would ultimately be air power that would be the decisive factor in achieving Nixon's objective—a negotiated end to the war for the United States.

Nixon's Thump and Talk Strategy

Although Nixon had campaigned in 1968 on a promise to bring the war to a quick end, he and his national security adviser Henry Kissinger were not about to hand the North Vietnamese an easy victory. From their perspective the American exodus from Vietnam had to be carefully stage-managed. It needed to avoid negative repercussions for the Cold War rivalry with the Soviet Union and China, to ensure American credibility in the world and for its global security commitments, and to preserve domestic support for the President. Nixon, being the ultimate political animal, ended up adopting a two-prong strategy that would aggressively pursue military victory on the battlefield, while at the same time continuing to negotiate with Hanoi.

Under the mantle of achieving "peace with honor," the Nixon administration moved forward by laying the groundwork for an escalation of the war through the secret bombing of North Vietnamese and Viet Cong bases in Cambodia. Under Operation Menu, various sub-operations were directed against logistics, support, and command and control centers along the Cambodian–South Vietnamese border. The first covert B-52 strikes began on March 18, 1969. Both sides refused to publicly acknowledge the bombing; Washington was fearful of alarming the American public and fueling more anti-war sentiment and Hanoi did not want to admit it was operating from bases inside "neutral" Cambodia. The attacks would continue for the next 15 months at varying levels up until the ground invasion of Cambodia by American and ARVN forces in May 1970.

Southeast Asia Theater of Operations.

Above left: President Richard Nixon and his national security adviser Henry Kissinger sought to disengage the United States from Vietnam while ensuring the viability of South Vietnam and maintaining U.S. global credibility in the face of an unpopular war. (Photo Nixon Library)

Above right: General Creighton Abrams, as commander U.S. Military Assistance Command, Vietnam (MACV) from 1968 to 1972, was charged with overseeing the drawdown of American ground troops while still continuing to prosecute the war. (Photo U.S. Army)

The bombing campaign accomplished several of Nixon's objectives early on, even if it had little long-term impact on the actual fighting in South Vietnam. First and foremost, it signaled the new administration's willingness to take aggressive, and even unpredictable, military action against Hanoi. Second, the bombing provided a relatively low-risk approach that avoided any significant commitment of the remaining American ground forces. This in turn allowed publicly announced troop withdrawals to continue, which not only placated anti-war sentiment at home, but provided tangible evidence that Washington was open to a negotiated settlement of the war. Finally, the bombing aligned with the long-standing desire of General Creighton Abrams, commander U.S. Military Assistance Command, Vietnam (MACV), to disrupt North Vietnamese operations by targeting their safe havens and lines of communication in Cambodia and buy time to strengthen the South Vietnamese military.

Nixon also sought to parlay the bombing of Cambodia into political leverage at the ongoing Paris peace talks. Using his so-called "madman strategy," Nixon wanted to convince Hanoi's leadership that the bombing was just a first step and unless the North de-escalated its military activity in the South and advanced the peace progress, much worse was to come. Nixon was a madman was the message. He is "obsessed about

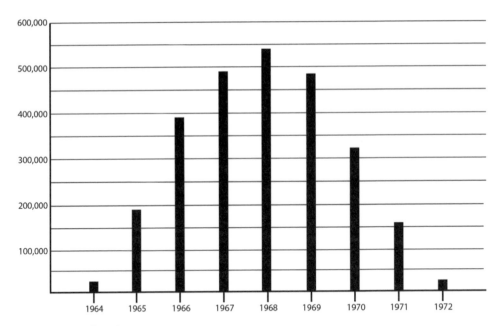

U.S. Troop Levels, 1964–1973.

Communists" and "can't be restrained when he's angry"[1] and will stop at nothing to end the war, including the bombing of North Vietnamese cities, a ground invasion across the DMZ or even the use of nuclear weapons unless Hanoi was willing to make concessions. Likewise, Kissinger thought the bombing could be used to signal the Soviets—the largest supplier of war matériel to North Vietnam—that unless Moscow used its influence over Hanoi things might get even more out of hand.[2] In addition, Kissinger was well aware of Moscow's desire to improve bilateral relations with the new administration and thus might be open to putting pressure on the North Vietnamese in return for American cooperation in advancing more important Cold War priorities. In the end, he and Nixon were gambling that global geostrategic considerations would ultimately trump any allegiance to socialist solidarity.

While Nixon's tough stance forced both Hanoi and Moscow to reassess their positions, the fighting in South Vietnam still continued unabated. Likewise, peace talks in Paris dragged on into 1970 without making any significant progress. Apparently the time was not yet ripe for peace.

Betting on Vietnamization

By the beginning 1970, the Nixon administration had gone all in on its policy of Vietnamization—whereby responsibility for combat operations and the defense of South Vietnam would pass from American to Vietnamese hands—and it would be here that the fate of America's disengagement would be staked. Under Secretary of Defense Melvin Laird's direction the United States sought to equip, train, and create a South Vietnamese military that would be capable of "assuming full responsibility for the security of South

Vietnam."[3] Secretary Laird, a strong advocate of the strategy, estimated that when the program began in March 1969 it would take at least three years to accomplish the task.[4] In the meantime, the more than half a million American troops in Vietnam would start to reduce their direct ground combat role and increasingly turn this responsibility over to South Vietnamese units as part of a phased withdrawal of U.S. forces. Critical logistics and combat support functions—most notably air and fire support missions— would, however, remain largely in the hands of the Americans for the foreseeable future. In addition, the administration warned that any escalating North Vietnamese aggression would jeopardize American troop drawdowns and that the United States was prepared "to take strong and effective [military] measures" in response.[5]

On paper Vietnamization appeared to be the answer that would provide the military and political leverage to end the war that Washington was seeking. It would buy time for the Americans to reach an acceptable peace agreement with Hanoi while limiting U.S. casualties. It would undercut the U.S. anti-war movement's calls for a quick unilateral withdrawal of all troops. It would create an independent South Vietnamese military counterweight capable of stalemating the North Vietnamese on the battlefield. Most important, however, was Kissinger's belief that continuing North Vietnamese intransigence in reaching a peace settlement would only worsen Hanoi's military situation in the South, as it "permits the United States to carry out Vietnamization at its own pace."[6] This dilemma he reasoned should be prime motivation for Hanoi to quit its delaying tactics at the peace talks.[7] Thus, the Americans energetically moved forward on building one of the largest and best-equipped militaries in the world in South Vietnam, one that would ultimately boast over a million men under arms, more than 1,000 aircraft, and 1,680 naval craft by 1972.[8]

Secretary of Defense Melvin Laird, the architect of the Vietnamization program.

Reality, however, would prove to be a harsh mistress for the Americans' Vietnamization strategy and there were warning signs early on. Despite making steady progress in the arming and training of South Vietnamese forces, the quality of many of the new units remained suspect as extensive corruption, personal rivalries, and poor leadership hamstrung the development of an effective and professional officer cadre. Likewise, an over-reliance on American firepower support to come to the rescue of beleaguered units created a level of dependence and unrealistic expectations that was all but impossible to maintain as Washington drew down its forces. All these factors would become the program's Achilles heel and it was only a matter of time before Vietnamization was put to the test.

The first test came at the end of April 1970 when Nixon ordered a joint U.S.–South Vietnamese cross-border strike into Cambodia to shore up support for Prime Minister Lon Nol's newly installed government. Lon Nol had recently assumed power following a March coup d'état by a pro-Western faction of Cambodian military and civilian elites when they ousted Prince Norodom Sihanouk from power. A central grievance of theirs was Prince Sihanouk's willingness to tolerate the unfettered presence of North Vietnamese troops and bases on Cambodian soil. Efforts to remove the North Vietnamese quickly turned into disaster as the Cambodian army faced battle-hardened troops and soon Lon Nol's government was on the verge of collapse. Fearful of the situation spinning out of control and Kissinger's concern that "the United States could not stand by and watch Cambodia collapse and ultimately cause the collapse of the U.S. effort in Vietnam," Nixon ordered General Abrams to take quick and decisive action to reverse the situation.[9] On April 30 American and South Vietnamese units numbering nearly 25,000 men crossed the Cambodian border to drive the estimated 40,000 North Vietnamese and Viet Cong from their sanctuaries, destroy their supplies, and disrupt their operations. The primary target areas were the Parrot's Beak and Fishhook salients that jutted into Vietnamese territory and were located less than 50 miles northwest of Saigon. Nixon defended his decision to the American people as necessary "to protect our men who are in Vietnam and to guarantee the continued success of our withdrawal and Vietnamization programs."[10] Nonetheless, the invasion sparked massive anti-war protests in the United States.

The incursions would last approximately three months and were declared a success for not only achieving their operational goals of disrupting North Vietnamese staging areas and capturing or destroying large amounts of war matériel, but as to the success of Vietnamization. Certainly many South Vietnamese units performed well, but few casualties were inflicted as the enemy simply slipped away deeper into Cambodia and the entire command and control structure escaped intact. Moreover, ARVN forces were often too content to have U.S. firepower pound their objectives before advancing and failed to face any substantial resistance. They—and the success of Vietnamization—were far from proven.

The real test would come less than a year later in early February 1971 when the South Vietnamese launched Operation Lon Sam 719. The operation was designed to strike a key North Vietnamese–Viet Cong logistic center and interdict the flow of supplies coming down the Ho Chi Minh Trail in southern Laos. U.S. congressional restrictions following Nixon's Cambodia foray the previous year made it illegal to use any American

President Nixon provides a public briefing on April 30, 1970 of the American and South Vietnamese ground incursion into Cambodia. (Photo White House)

ground troops in the operation. With the exception of American close air cover and helicopter resupply missions, the ARVN would be on its own. The plan concocted by MACV called for a roughly 6,000-man force of South Vietnamese infantry and armor to drive some 25 miles into Laos along Route 9 to capture the town of Tchepone, which served as the logistics hub, destroying supplies and thwarting any communist preoffensive build-up in the area.

Things began to go awry from the start. The slow pace of the advance gave the North Vietnamese time to call in reinforcements and stiffen their resistance. The heavy armored column of tanks and artillery became bogged down and was unable to maneuver off the confining road and river valley, presenting inviting targets for North Vietnamese artillery. After advancing only 12 miles the ARVN forces dug in and called upon U.S. air support to stem the increasingly aggressive enemy counterattacks against its flanks. The Americans responded, but poor coordination and confusion on the ground hindered the effectiveness of airstrikes. As South Vietnamese casualties mounted, President Nguyen Van Thieu scaled back the operation and announced a complete withdrawal in late March after the symbolic capture of Tchepone. Nixon was furious. Lam Son 719 he believed was "our last opportunity to achieve a significant long-range benefit from large offensive operations."[11] It didn't matter. Thieu and the ARVN had had enough. To make matters worse the withdrawal quickly turned into a disorderly rout and many battle-weary units broke and fled. Pictures of ARVN soldiers clinging to the skids of departing American helicopters were soon flashing around the globe.

South Vietnamese troops equipped with American armored personnel carriers advance toward the Cambodian border, April 1970.

Nevertheless, the White House sought to portray the operation as a qualified success by claiming it blunted a planned North Vietnamese offensive in 1971, inflicted more than 9,000 enemy dead, destroyed nearly 14,000 tons of munitions, and captured or destroyed thousands of weapons, including over a hundred tanks.[12] Politically, Nixon sought to assuage the American public by claiming that "the South Vietnamese [had] demonstrated that without American advisers they could fight effectively against the very best troops North Vietnam could put in the field."[13] This allowed him to announce the drawdown of an additional 100,000 troops by the end of the year. This would leave a little more than 150,000 troops—less than 20 percent of which were combat troops—in South Vietnam by December 1971. The ground war was quickly becoming a purely Vietnamese affair.

Peace Talks Drag On

Even as the war in Southeast Asia raged on and each side sought to gain the upper hand on the battlefield, both Washington and Hanoi continued their diplomatic dance in Paris. Albeit at a snail's pace. By January 1972, three years of back and forth between the Americans and North Vietnamese had failed to advance the cause of peace. While secret meetings regularly took place between Kissinger and North Vietnamese negotiators Le Duc Tho and Xuan Thuy, each side stuck rigidly to its position with little room for compromise. Critically, both sides firmly believed that the advantage was still on their side. A settlement would have to wait.

The Paris Peace Process

Even as the fighting continued to rage on the battlefields of South Vietnam in the aftermath of the 1968 Tet Offensive and American planes continued to rain down bombs on the North, U.S. and North Vietnamese representatives began meeting in Paris on May 13, 1968 to discuss a negotiated end to the conflict—although neither side was really ready to make the necessary concessions or compromises needed to advance the cause of peace at that time.

President Lyndon Johnson, who now believed the war was unwinnable and announced in March his public intention not to run for reelection and to de-escalate the war, saw the Paris talks as his one last political opportunity to negotiate the United States out of a war that had spiraled out of his control. The North Vietnamese leadership was more circumspect about engaging in talks. For despite the terrible military setbacks Hanoi had suffered during the year, it saw American resolve beginning to weaken and that gave the North optimism. Moreover, uncertainty over how the negotiations might play out given the past experience with the Geneva Accords in 1954 made First Secretary Le Duan very wary. Battlefield gains in the war with the French had been sacrificed for political expediency. Le Duan was not about to repeat that mistake. So his close confidant and reliable deputy, Le Du Tho, was appointed a "special adviser" to the talks.

So began more than four years of on again-off again negotiations in Paris. More often than not, they were little more than political theater or a venue for espousing propaganda to assuage the international community of each side's commitment to peace. Entrenched positions, such as Hanoi's demand for the removal of President Thieu or Washington's requirement that all North Vietnamese troops leave the South, left little room for compromise. Moreover, both sides continued to pursue dual-track strategies of seeking a military advantage on the battlefield to buttress their bargaining position at the talks. Thus, by 1970 the Nixon administration believed that Vietnamization would push Hanoi to seek a deal with Washington rather than be faced with the prospect of dealing with a strengthened, U.S.-supported regime in Saigon once American troops left the country. In contrast, Le Duan and his politburo allies believed that one final military push just might be enough to topple the Thieu government, forcing Washington to accept Hanoi's terms or face the prospect of returning to the battlefield.

Meanwhile behind the scenes, both sides were under increasing pressure to strike a compromise by 1972. Strong anti-war sentiment in the United States and growing congressional restrictions on the military in Vietnam, as well as the drawdown in American forces greatly constrained President Nixon's ability to threaten Hanoi. Deep-seated concerns by U.S. military advisers and some White House officials over the ability of South Vietnamese forces to stand on their own put the ultimate success of the Vietnamization strategy in doubt. Despite President Thieu's reelection in 1971, the Saigon regime remained as divided, fragile, and unpopular as even. The picture wasn't much better from Hanoi's viewpoint either. The American policy of détente with the Soviet Union and rapprochement with China made the North increasing vulnerable to the broader foreign policy agendas of Moscow and Beijing. Even more disconcerting, the widening Sino-Soviet split forced Hanoi to strike a delicate political balance or face a potential cut-off in vital sources of military assistance. Although still welding a firm hand over the party in the wake of Ho Chi Minh's death in 1969, Le Duan and his allies were on shaky ground. Repeated efforts to foment a popular uprising in the South through large-scale military offensives had failed miserably and at great cost in men and equipment.

The stars for peace would finally begin to align in the fall of 1972, but this was only after both sides had their mettle tested once again on the battlefields of South Vietnam and in the skies over the North Vietnamese heartland. The pressure on Hanoi and Washington became too much not to make peace—even if it was only the illusion of peace. What wasn't possible in October now seemed inevitable in early 1973. The signing of the Paris Peace Accords on January 25, 1973 officially ended America's military role in the Vietnam War. From then on it would be up to the Vietnamese people to finally determine their own fate.

Central to the North's calculation was its perception of the war. From Hanoi's view the conflict with the South was one essentially over the fate and future of Vietnamese nationalism. The Americans were the "outsiders" and not the North Vietnamese. Thus, any discussion of a ceasefire based on a mutual withdrawal of forces was a non-starter; even more so because Hanoi patently refused to acknowledge that it had *any troops* in the South at all.[14] Hanoi was also firm in its demand that President Thieu and his regime be removed from office in any settlement to the war—a condition that was naturally unacceptable to the Americans. Washington was also firm in its insistence that the final removal of its forces be conditioned on the release of all American prisoners of war held by the North Vietnamese and Viet Cong.

Further hindering progress was the belief by both sides that time was on their side, and thus delaying could be beneficial in extracting concessions from the other. Hanoi for its part had always seen the conflict with the Washington as a war of attrition. The Vietnamese had outlasted the Chinese, Japanese, and French. Now it was the Americans' turn. "If the war continues," Tho told Kissinger, "we are firmly confident of our success, in our victory."[15] And although anxious to disengage from Vietnam, the Nixon White House was in no hurry to give the country away to the communists. Vietnamization, as problematic as it was, would buy Washington time to stave off defeat on the battlefield. Thanks to the twin pillars of ongoing phased troop withdrawals and the Vietnamization program, Nixon believed he had some domestic room to maneuver now that he had undercut the anti-war movement. Kissinger too sought to use the delays as leverage against Hanoi

Henry Kissinger and Le Duc Tho were charged by their respective governments to negotiate a diplomatic solution to ending the war that both Washington and Hanoi would find acceptable.

by playing up the newfound Soviet and Chinese desire for improved relations with the United States. His point was driven home when Nixon made his historic visit to Beijing in February 1972 and then to Moscow two months later.

With neither party willing to make meaningful concessions and under no pressure to do so, both Hanoi and Washington would turn their attention once again to the battlefield to break the deadlock. For the North it would be in South Vietnam. For the United States it would be in the skies over North Vietnam. Although few could have foreseen it at the time, 1972 was shaping up as a year of decision for both—but not in the way either had expected.

2. THE YEAR OF THE RAT—A TIME OF DECISION

As the American war in Vietnam dragged into its eighth year, U.S. battlefield deaths had fallen to ten per week (down from an average of 280 per week in 1968), troop levels were slated to fall to below 65,000, and the burden of fighting had shifted to the Saigon regime thanks to the Vietnamization program.[1] Americans were tired of the war, a war that was increasingly being pushed to the backburner of their concern, yet it was no closer to being resolved.

With peace talks deadlocked in Paris, both sides sought to tactfully bolster their negotiating position on the battlefield. For Washington this meant continuing to militarily strengthen the capability of President Thieu's government to survive on its own, while also threatening retaliation should Hanoi escalate its attacks. For Hanoi this meant accelerating its buildup of forces and supplies in Cambodia, Laos, and the southern panhandle of North Vietnam in preparation for going over on to the offensive once the time was right—the South Vietnamese still too weak to stop them and the Americans too ill-disposed to return to the battlefield. By all calculations the Vietnamese zodiac calendar's Year of the Rat that began on February 15, 1972 was shaping up as a time of decision.

The View from Washington

Despite the lackluster pace of peace talks amid the seeming intransigence of the North Vietnamese, President Nixon was far from ready to throw in the towel. Yes, the administration wanted out of Vietnam as it promised the American people. Yes, the American public was tired of the war and ready to move on. And yes, the Congress was increasingly reluctant to fund what seemed like an open-ended commitment to the Saigon government, which appeared to be as weak and feeble as ever despite hundreds of billions of dollars in U.S. military and economic assistance. Nonetheless, for Nixon and Kissinger the price of failing to obtain "peace with honor" in Southeast Asia was too high a political cost to incur and as long as they were willing to prevent the North from gaining a victory on the battlefield there was hope of success at the negotiating table. It was a supreme test of wills. It was also a dangerous gamble.

The Nixon White House was willing to take this risk, because it believed the future credibility of American

South Vietnamese President Nguyen Van Thieu proved to be a constant thorn in the side of American efforts throughout 1971–72 to negotiate a peace settlement and only relented when backed into a corner by Nixon and Kissinger.

foreign policy and global leadership was at stake. Any resolution of the conflict in Vietnam that damaged or negatively affected American standing in the world was unacceptable. Nixon and Kissinger saw themselves as operating on a global stage beyond Southeast Asia. Détente with the Soviet Union, arms control, revamping the Sino-American relationship, and stemming conflict in the Middle East were the new priorities for the Nixon White House. Vietnam had been President Lyndon Johnson's problem, but it was not going to be theirs. Cold, hard political calculus revealed that American military disengagement from Vietnam after 1968 was the only option left; it was only a question of the manner and the timing.

The role of international diplomacy and American grand strategy was also seen as critical in Washington's ability to pressure Hanoi into make concessions. By leveraging the prospect of improving relations with the Moscow and Beijing, the Nixon administration sought to isolate North Vietnam. The loss of Soviet or Chinese support—or even the perception of pending loss—might be just enough to force Hanoi's hand at the peace talks. Moreover, a closer relationship with either benefactor would likely reduce the chances of a strident reaction from Moscow or Beijing should the United States choose to unleash massive military force directly against the North Vietnamese. While high-profile American summit diplomacy failed to break the negotiation logjam in early 1972, the message was clearly not lost on Hanoi: old alliances are vulnerable, the world is changing.

In the meantime, fearful that Hanoi would increasingly seek to take advantage of the American troop drawdown to shift the balance on the battlefield in the South, the administration was forced to rely on tailored military force to affirm its resolve and burnish the political position of the Thieu government. By late 1971, however, Washington had become nearly entirely dependent on air power to signal its displeasure with Hanoi and to counter provocative North Vietnamese military activity outside of South Vietnam. This U.S. air effort took two primary approaches: interdiction of the Ho Chi Minh Trail through intensive bombing and the launching of "protective reaction strikes" into North Vietnam.

President Nixon sought to honor his 1968 election pledge to draw down U.S. ground combat forces in South Vietnam, despite fears by many of his military commanders that Hanoi would seize the opportunity to pursue victory over Saigon on the battlefield.

Stopping, or at least slowing, the steady stream of men and matériel infiltrating into South Vietnam from the North had long been an essential element of American counterinsurgency strategy from day one. Accordingly, Washington committed extensive manpower, equipment, and technology from 1965 onward in an attempt to interdict the Ho Chi Minh Trail. This proved to be a Herculean task. With its vast array of jungle trails, improvised roads, makeshift bridges, and waystations that ran through the southern Laotian panhandle and into eastern Cambodia, it was a next to impossible assignment to accomplish. This was not for want of trying. Vast swaths of the Laotian jungle were under constant aerial reconnaissance and more than 20,000 highly sophisticated seismic and acoustic sensors were eventually seeded along infiltration routes.[2] As part of Operation Commando Hunt, U.S. aircraft, including heavy B-52 bombers, subjected key road junctions, mountain passes, bridges, and hidden supply depots and logistics support facilities to relentless day and night bombing. Meanwhile, patrolling AC-130 and AC-119 aircraft along with helicopter gunships sought out vehicular traffic for destruction. The missions were not without their risks, as beefed-up North Vietnamese air defenses, including the first confirmed presence of SA-2 surface-to-air missiles in April 1971, took a rising toll on American aircraft. By the end of the year it was estimated that the North Vietnamese had some 550 anti-aircraft guns deployed in Laos.[3] A total of 26 Air Force and Navy aircraft were lost in 1971; 24 pilots and crewmen were killed and another six taken prisoner.[4] In addition, the effort was estimated to be costing the United States about $2 billion a year.[5]

Unfortunately, the results were not always commensurate with the effort, which provoked an ongoing debate. There were sharp disagreements as to Commando Hunt's effectiveness. The Air Force claimed the operation was destroying about 60 percent of the supplies transiting southern Laos, while the CIA estimated the figure at only 20–25 percent.[6] Moreover, many in the intelligence community believed that given the relatively low logistics requirements to maintain enemy forces in the field, any reduced flow of supplies through Laos was likely to have little impact on the level of enemy activity in the South. The Joint Chiefs of Staff countered this by saying that any "hampering of the flow of men and supplies ... greatly restricted enemy initiatives and in some cases forced him to forego planned operations."[7] MACV even went so far as to say that the interdiction effort "took a serious toll of Communist trucks and supplies, thereby preventing any generally sustained ground activity by the enemy in 1971."[8] Like many contentious issues this one would not be resolved, but rather be over taken by events in the early months of 1972.

The other pillar of American air power was the use of "protective reaction strikes." Originally intended as retaliation for Hanoi's harassing attacks against U.S. reconnaissance aircraft overflying North Vietnam following the 1968 bombing halt, these reactive strikes increasingly came to be seen by the Nixon administration as an important tool in pressuring Hanoi both diplomatically and militarily. In point of fact, with the declining American military presence in Southeast Asia, Washington had few options left for flexing its muscles.

The result, however, was an escalating spiral of reprisals by both sides. Hanoi, unwilling to let this aggression go unchallenged, shifted stronger air defenses—including radar-controlled 85-mm anti-aircraft guns and SA-2 batteries—southward toward the demilitarized

The Laotian Air War

By the early 1970s the civil war in Laos between the Western-supported Royal Laotian forces and the North Vietnamese-supported Pathet Lao communist insurgents was entering its third decade. And since the mid-1960s it had become a venue for a de facto proxy war between Washington and Hanoi, one that would serve as a major theater of U.S. air operations right up until the very end of the America's Vietnam involvement.

Operation Barrel Roll was the first U.S. air interdiction operation and grew out of a plea by the Royal Lao government for assistance in slowing the flow of supply to Pathet Lao forces from North Vietnam. In December 1964, President Lyndon Johnson secretly authorized limited American airstrikes in the northeast border area of Laos and North Vietnam. The Air Force and Navy, operating from bases in Thailand, South Vietnam, and the Gulf of Tonkin, employed a wide variety of strike aircraft, including B-52 bombers, to attack enemy supply depots, bridges, and transportation routes. In addition, American air power was used periodically to stem Pathet Lao offensives. Although the bombing had only marginal military impact on the Laotian civil war, it provided a strong psychological boost to the Royal Lao government. Barrel Roll finally came to an end in February 1973 when the United States completed its withdrawal from Vietnam.

By the end of 1964 the Laotian panhandle, which contained the Ho Chi Minh Trail and other North Vietnamese infiltration routes, had become part of a major conduit into South Vietnam. To counter this flow of men and supply Johnson authorized Operation Steel Tiger in April 1965. By mid-1965 the Americans were flying 1,000 sorties per month as part of the interdiction effort and by 1967 that number had increased to more than 3,000, over half of which were large B-52 strikes. Air Force AC-130 and AC-119 gunships were also used extensively with devastating effect against truck and troop convoys. A subsidiary operation, Tiger Hound, covered the far southern Laotian panhandle adjacent to the five northern provinces of South Vietnam as part of General William Westmoreland's extended battlefield and fell under his control.

In 1968 the air interdiction effort against the Ho Chi Minh Trail in Laos was consolidated into a single new effort, Operation Commando Hunt, which lasted until January 1973. The difficult jungle terrain, North Vietnamese concealment techniques, and the tireless repair efforts of hundreds of thousands of laborers often limited the effectiveness of the bombing. Moreover, despite claiming to have destroyed tens of thousands of trucks, huge quantities of ammunition and supplies, and killed or wounded a large number of enemy troops, the American effort had only a marginal impact on the North's ability to prosecute the war in the South or limit its ability to mount large-scale offensives.

General John Lavelle as commander of the Seventh Air Force since August 1971 sought to pursue an aggressive retaliatory air strategy against the North, but found himself caught up in a political whirlwind that cost him his job and career. (Photo U.S. Air Force)

zone (DMZ) and closer to the Laotian border. By early 1971 American and allied aircraft operating over Laos and south of the DMZ were subject to mounting air defense fire. This elicited several large-scale protective reactive strikes by Air Force and Navy aircraft in February and March, involving more than 300 strike sorties and flying missions deep into North Vietnamese territory.[9] Vietnamese People's Air Force (VPAF) fighter aircraft also began penetrating Lao airspace in April 1971, posing a new threat to U.S. aircraft operating there. Photo reconnaissance also showed refurbishment of several older VPAF airfields south of the 19th parallel, including at Quang Lang adjacent to the border with Laos.

As the year progressed the size and frequency of U.S. retaliatory strikes steadily rose in response to these new threats. In December, higher command authority urged field commanders to be more aggressive and flexible interpreting existing restrictions. Soon after the General John Lavelle, the Seventh Air Force commander, began to adopt a "more vigorous protective reaction posture."[10] The first three months of 1972 saw more than 90 protective reaction strikes launched, compared to 108 during all of the previous year in what was quickly evolving into a new de facto bombing campaign.[11]

The opportunity to take advantage of looser rules of engagement to launch, what were in effect, preemptive strikes into North Vietnam came at a critical moment for the United States. With the Paris talks going nowhere, it appeared that Hanoi was increasingly willing to let the momentum of the U.S. troop withdrawal and American anti-war sentiment box Nixon into a corner. And despite the bellicose rhetoric coming out of Washington, there was no turning back on Vietnamization and stricter U.S. congressional oversight of the war in the aftermath of the secret bombing of Cambodia and the 1970 incursions gave Nixon little military leverage. This left him with few options other than the escalation of protective reaction strikes. Moreover, this use of air power had several advantages. First, it allowed Nixon and Kissinger to forcefully remind Hanoi that the war was far from over in the hope of reinvigorating the peace talks. Second, it had the military benefit of disrupting North Vietnamese offensive preparations, while also signaling ever more fierce retaliation should the North escalate its activities. Finally, it permitted the administration to tacitly circumvent congressional opposition to any expansion of American military action north of the DMZ. All this was important as it seemed merely a matter of time before Hanoi was likely to take advantage of the declining American military presence to test the mettle of Saigon's forces.

The View From Hanoi

For the senior North Vietnamese leadership, 1972 was indeed shaping up well, a year that they believed would see the realization of their longstanding dream of freeing the Vietnamese people from foreign rule and influence once and for all. Since the death of Ho Chi Minh in September 1969, power within North Vietnam had become concentrated in the hands of Secretary General Le Duan, Prime Minister Pham Van Dong, and General Vo Nguyen Giap, all of whom were ardent nationalists united in their commitment to defeating the United States. They were, however, also pragmatists. The defeat of the Americans could come either on the battlefield or at the negotiating table. Thus, for the past several years they pursued their own version of a fight and talk strategy that sought political concessions from the Americans in Pairs, while also preparing to militarily defeat the United States and its Saigon ally on the battlefield.

Now it seemed that the stars were beginning to align in mid-February 1972 as the Year of the Rat began. With Nixon facing reelection in the face of an unpopular war, North Vietnamese leaders reasoned that his hands would be increasingly tied by domestic political considerations. Likewise, the White House's public commitment to de-escalating the war through troop withdrawals and the small size of the remaining U.S. forces in Vietnam

The powerful Secretary General of the Vietnamese Communist party, Le Duan, gambled on achieving a military victory by launching the Easter Offensive on March 30, 1972 rather than pursue a negotiated settlement to the war with the Americans.

would likely limit Washington's ability to respond militarily. And even if the Americans resorted to bombing of the North again as they had threatened, the North Vietnamese had weathered the storm before during Operation Rolling Thunder and could do it again. Besides the Soviets and Chinese were likely to denounce any renewed bombing campaign and put diplomatic pressure on the Americans to stop it.

Militarily things were looking up for Hanoi too. Its forces and logistics network in Cambodia had been reconstituted since the 1970 U.S.-South Vietnamese incursions and were ready along with their Viet Cong allies to go over to the offensive. American air interdiction efforts over southern Laos and the North Vietnamese panhandle, as well as Operation Lam Son 719, had caused some disruptions, but not enough to prevent Hanoi from being able to amass large numbers of men and matériel along the South Vietnamese border. In addition, the poor performance of ARVN troops during Lam Son 719 not only boosted the confidence of the North Vietnamese Army (NVA) in its ability to go toe to toe with the ARVN and win, but it validated Hanoi's belief in the failure of Vietnamization.[12]

Not surprisingly then, in mid-1971 the politburo of the North Vietnamese communist party had determined that "the time has come to bring about a favorable moment" and "intensify our struggle" [through military action to] achieve a decisive victory in the year 1972 and compel the American imperialists to end the war through negotiations on our terms."[13] Accordingly, military planning for a general offensive—along the lines of the 1968 Tet Offensive—to strike a crushing blow against the Saigon government kicked into high gear. After approving the plan, which called for a large-scale conventional assault using tanks and heavy artillery into the northern provinces of South Vietnam combined with diversionary attacks in the far south and central highlands, the politburo was increasingly confident of victory. The objective of the offensive would be to capture and hold the northern provinces of South Vietnam while engaging and destroying large numbers of South Vietnamese troops. This in turn would lead to the complete collapse of Saigon's military and the implosion of the regime.

Since the end of Rolling Thunder and the bombing halt in November 1968 Hanoi had steadily and systematically rebuilt the North's transportation, industrial, and military infrastructure. By the early 1970s, Hanoi was working feverishly to improve its logistic capability, strengthen its air defenses, stockpile supplies and equipment, and create new troop staging areas across the southern panhandle. Petroleum pipelines were being built through the Mu Gia Pass on the Laotian border and to just north of the DMZ and construction was also underway to extend the North Vietnamese road network into South Vietnamese territory.[14] Work on improving the airfields at Quang Lang, Vinh, and Dong Hoi was in progress too. Thus, Hanoi's southern panhandle was fast becoming a well-equipped and -defended arsenal, bristling with growing numbers of men and equipment.

This changing situation was not lost on the Americans. With a new sense of urgency Washington ordered a number of large-scale preemptive strikes against this build-up. Operation Prize Bull was launched on September 21, 1971 during which 196 aircraft stuck POL (petroleum, oil and lubricants) storage facilities south of the 19th parallel and destroyed an estimated 470,000 gallons of capacity and starting several huge fires.[15] Following several attempts by VPAF MiGs to intercept and shoot down B-52s operating over Laos in October, U.S. Air Force and Navy planes also attacked the airfields at

The North Vietnamese politburo seriously underestimated the political will of Washington and capability of American air power to respond forcefully to Hanoi's aggression in the South. (Photo Naval History and Heritage Command)

Quang Lang, Vinh, and Dong Hoi in early November. The White House publicly claimed that these were simply retaliatory strikes, but the Pentagon tacitly acknowledged that the bombing was also being done "with an eye toward stopping any major buildup before it develops."[16] Hanoi was being put on notice.

As if to remove any sense of pretext as to what was evolving into an American interdiction effort over the North Vietnamese panhandle, Operation Proud Deep Alpha was

The Lavelle Affair

Since the end of Operation Rolling Thunder in November 1968, U.S. air operations over North Vietnam became limited to reconnaissance collection missions with accompanying fighter escorts. Moreover, under highly restrictive rules of engagement American aircraft undertaking these missions were only permitted to defensively respond to "hostile actions" directed against them. They were strictly prohibited from initiating any offensive actions. By late 1971, however, American aircraft overflying North Vietnam and those conducting air operations in neighboring Laos found themselves under increasing threat as Hanoi built up its air defenses in the southern panhandle of North Vietnam. In the final three weeks of December alone ten aircraft and 13 crewmen were lost over southern Laos. Reconnaissance flights over the North also found themselves facing a growing threat south of the 19th parallel from newly established surface-to-air missiles sites, a rising number of anti-aircraft guns, and increasingly aggressive MiG fighters.

To counter this threat and send a message to Hanoi, the Joint Chiefs urged Air Force and Navy field commanders to be more aggressive and flexible in interpreting the existing rules of engagement. Authorization was also given in December 1971 to increase the number of fighter escorts on reconnaissance missions from two to eight or even 16 if need be "to insure adequate damage" to enemy defenses when fired upon. General John Lavelle, commander of the Seventh Air Force since August, saw this as endorsement of higher command authority to escalate protective reaction strikes over the southern panhandle of North Vietnam. Thus, not only were the offending air defense sites to be attacked, but associated airfields, radars, SA-2 missile transports, fuel supplies, and ammo dumps became fair game. According to General Lavelle, "We went in after these targets, the ones that would hurt the enemy's defensive system, so that we could operate." These "ad hoc" reactive airstrikes were in addition to a growing number of planned larger scale protective reaction strikes, like December's Proud Deep Alpha operation, in what was quickly becoming a new air campaign over North Vietnam's southern panhandle by 1972.

Back channel reports of Lavelle's "unauthorized bombing" of the North came to light in early March 1972 and resulted in a congressional inquiry. A subsequent investigation by the Air Force Inspector General determined that Lavelle had conducted 28 unauthorized missions, consisting of 147 sorties, as well as finding out that that the Seventh Air Force had deliberately falsified reports to hide the activity. Air Force Chief of Staff General John Ryan immediately recalled Lavelle in April, telling him of his plans to relieve him of command. This effectively ended Lavelle's career and he chose to retire at the rank of major general. Lavelle was replaced by General John Vogt as the Seventh Air Force commander on April 10.

Lavelle consistently defend his actions, telling congressional leaders that he believed he was acting on orders from higher command and that the charges were "a catastrophic blemish" on his military record "for conscientiously doing the job I was expected to do." Nonetheless, General Ryan and the Chairman of the Joint Chiefs, Admiral Thomas Moorer, testified that they were unaware of any falsified reports and that Lavelle was not encouraged—officially or unofficially—to stretch the rules of engagement. The White House also publicly said his actions were not authorized and "it was proper for him to be relieved and retired." In 2007, however, the discovery of White House recordings from the Nixon archives showed that President Nixon had indeed authorized the bombing and that Nixon and Henry Kissinger struggled with the decision to make the White House's involvement public. "I don't want him [Lavelle] to be made a goat, god damn it. Frankly, Henry, I don't feel right [about this] and "I don't want to hurt an innocent man," said Nixon in a June 1972 recording. The potential political blowback, however, apparently proved too much for Nixon and Kissinger. Both remained silent. Thus, it turns out that Lavelle was right all along: he had been made a public scapegoat for a policy that was militarily sound, but politically insupportable.

Sources: J. Morrocco, *Rain of Fire*, pp. 104-105; *Washington Post*, August 5, 2010.

launched on December 26. The five-day operation—the largest series of airstrikes since the 1968 bombing halt—was designed to destroy MiG fighter aircraft on the ground and render the airfields at Quang Lang and Bai Thuong inoperable, while also targeting fuel and supply depots, SAM sites, and truck parks below the 20th parallel.[17] More than 1,000 sorties were flown, but poor weather hampered the effectiveness of the strikes. A number of POL storage facilities were moderately damaged and the runway at Quang Lang was heavily cratered. At least 45 SA-2 surface-to-air missiles were fired at the attackers and three struck home, resulting in the loss of an Air Force F-4D Phantom, a Navy F-4B Phantom, and a Navy A-6A Intruder.[18]

Likewise, two days of intense airstrikes in mid-February 1972 were launched to silence North Vietnamese long-range artillery just north of the DMZ that had begun shelling ARVN outposts to the south. In addition to attacking the artillery positions, logistics complexes and newly discovered SAM sites were also targeted. MACV claimed the attacks were successful in damaging or destroying seven 130-mm artillery pieces.[19] At least 81 SA-2 missiles were fired at the American attackers and two found their mark: an Air Force F-4D Phantom and an F-105G Wild Weasel (a specialized air defense suppression aircraft) were downed by the missiles and a third Air Force F-4D was lost to ground fire.[20] Despite the increasingly aggressive nature of American airstrikes and Washington's stern warning to Hanoi not to take advantage of the drawdown in U.S. forces, the North's preparations for the 1972 offensive continued unabated. The North Vietnamese were not about to be deterred; the die was clearly cast.

Despite ongoing U.S. and South Vietnamese interdiction efforts against the Ho Chi Minh Trail, Hanoi was able to amass several hundred thousand men and stockpile large amounts of supplies and military equipment along the borders of South Vietnam by early 1972.

The South Vietnamese incursion into southern Laos during Operation Lam Son 719 in early 1971 proved not only unsuccessful in significantly disrupting and destroying the enemy's logistics infrastructure and supplies, but demonstrated a weakness in Saigon's forces that Hanoi sought to exploit in the coming year.

The Easter Offensive Kicks Off

In the early morning hours of March 30, 1972 the still of the jungle was broken with the sound of tanks, heavy artillery, anti-aircraft guns, and some 40,000 NVA soldiers surging across the DMZ and eastern Laos into the northern South Vietnam. The invasion was on. In less than a week other North Vietnamese and Viet Cong units were crossing the border from the Parrot's Beak area of Cambodia to threaten strategic provinces north of Saigon. By mid-April government forces in the central highlands also found themselves under attack from NVA troops pouring across the Laotian border. In due course as many as 200,000 men along with T-54 main battle tanks, 130-mm towed artillery, ZSU-57 self-propelled anti-aircraft guns, and hundreds of trucks and armored personnel carriers were engaged across three battlefronts.[21] It was becoming increasingly apparent that Hanoi was intent on unleashing the largest and most sustained assault on U.S. and South Vietnamese forces in four years. It was surely a bold gamble by Hanoi, but the reward—if successful—was well worth the risk of ending the war in a single stroke.

Although not unexpected by any means, the sheer magnitude and breath of the "1972 Spring-Summer Offensive" (as the North Vietnamese called it) caught Saigon and Washington off guard, as did the willingness of NVA commanders to commit massed armored-infantry columns with supporting artillery and mobile air defense units to the

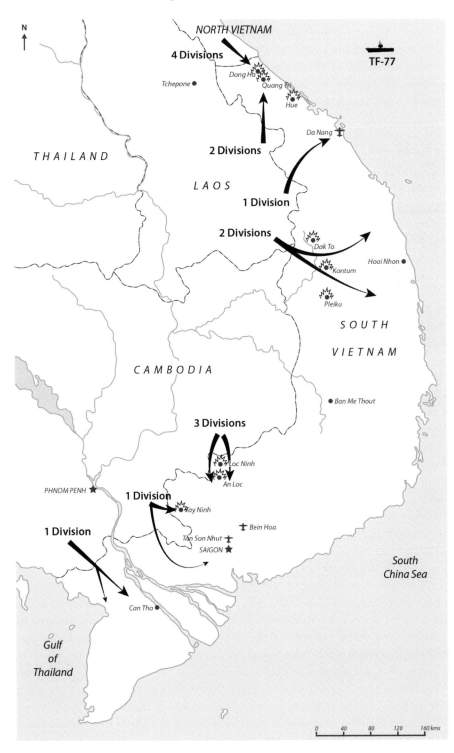

Easter Offensive, 1972.

fight. Under the weight of this conventional onslaught, many South Vietnamese units began to buckle and flee. Within a week ARVN bases south of the DMZ were completely overrun and a disorganized retreat toward the provincial capital of Quang Tri was underway. Heavy cloud cover and confusion on the ground prevented any effective U.S. or South Vietnamese Air Force (VNAF) response, but the timely arrival of South Vietnamese Marines and other ARVN reinforcements allowed resistance to stiffen just north of Quang Tri.

In the far south the town of Loc Ninh across the Cambodian border quickly fell on April 7 with the loss of more than two-thirds of its garrison. Soon the vitally important town of An Loc astride the main highway to Saigon was fighting for its life too. By April 12 the city was completely cut off and under heavy NVA mortar and artillery fire. The third prong of Hanoi's offensive saw dozens of government outposts and fire support bases in the central highlands overrun and by April 24 its forces were advancing on Kontum and Pleiku. By the end of the month Kontum was nearly surrounded and it was on the verge of falling.[22]

It was air power, however, that saved the day. Bad weather and poor visibility, lack of communications and coordination with ground forces severely hampered air operations in the early days of the offensive. Thus, NVA commanders took full advantage of the situation to press home their assaults and even brazenly took to open highways, driving fleeing ARVN soldiers and frightened civilians ahead of them. But as the weather improved and battle lines stabilized, American and South Vietnamese aircraft took to the skies to rain down torrents of bombs and hails of gunfire on the attacking columns. B-52 sorties rose dramatically from 700 in March to 1,600 in April to a peak of 2,000 in May.[23] Soon every available American plane and crew in Southeast Asia would be scrambled to stem the tide.

As the fighting at An Loc grew increasingly desperate, U.S. Air Force and Navy F-4s, along with VNAF A-1 Skyraiders and A-37 Dragonfly attack jets, relentlessly pounded attacking NVA infantry formations with napalm and 500-pound bombs. U.S. Army helicopter gunships also joined in by blasting enemy T-54 tanks with anti-tank rockets and waves of B-52 bombers out of Guam unloaded their massive payloads against enemy buildups on the outskirts of the city. Badly shattered, the remaining communist forces settled into a siege of the city by the end of the month.[24]

In the far north of the country, tactical airstrikes, artillery barrages, naval gunfire, and B-52 Arc Light strikes stiffened the resistance outside Quang Tri and slowed the enemy advance by inflicting heavy casualties.[25] Dozens of T-54 and PT-76 tanks were smoldering wrecks. Row after row of bomb craters littered the landscape approaching the city and hundreds of NVA soldiers lay dead on the battlefield. While overwhelming firepower bought time for the defenders, four weeks of fighting had taken its toll. The 3rd ARVN Division was completely mauled and ceased to exist. Abandoned artillery and other cast-off military equipment marked the line of retreat southward from the DMZ and even elite South Vietnamese Ranger and Marine units had their ranks decimated. There was very little left and on May 1 all resistance at Quang Tri collapsed. The ensuing retreat quickly became a rout in the chaos that followed. Intermingled fleeing troops and civilians were forced to run a gauntlet of enemy artillery and gun fire as they raced southward down coast Highway 1 to the promised safety of the old imperial capital of Hue. Only the bravery and determination of an ad hoc force of South Vietnamese Marines, Rangers, and

Above: A North Vietnamese heavy artillery battery unleashing a deadly barrage against South Vietnamese positions south of the DMZ as the Easter Offensive kicks off.

Below: In the space of a few weeks some 200,000 North Vietnamese and Viet Cong troops poured across the South Vietnamese border on three fronts, pushing the defenders to the brink of disaster.

tanks fighting a rearguard action staved off complete disaster.[26] On May 3 the last remnants crossed the Thac Ma River. Quang Tri Province was now completely in the hands of the North Vietnamese.

Things weren't much better in the central highlands either as the North Vietnamese closed in on Kontum in the early days of May. Meanwhile, other increasingly isolated central highlands outposts were simply abandoned with the defenders leaving artillery, munitions, and mountains of supplies behind. Unfortunately, this forced tactical airstrikes to be diverted to destroy the equipment and supplies before they fell into enemy hands. Once again it was air power that came to the rescue of the beleaguered forces with VNAF and U.S. aircraft, including AC-130E Spectre gunships with their 40-mm and 20-mm mini-guns, blasting massing troop formations to break up their assaults. B-52 strikes were also used as close-in support, often dropping their loads within 1,000 meters of friendly troops. All this proved extremely devastating and by one estimate 40 percent of the NVA force attacking Kontum was killed by May 14.[27]

In addition to flying tactical air support missions, both American and South Vietnamese aircraft played an equally crucial role in the first six weeks of the offensive by resupplying embattled garrisons and rushing reinforcements to the battle. Moreover, the role of cargo transport crews in braving intense small-arms and anti-aircraft fire—including the first use of the shoulder-fired SA-7 Strela surface-to-air missiles—proved to be decisive in the defense of both An Loc and Kontum. This was not without cost: three C-130 Hercules transports were lost to ground fire over An Loc during the siege of the city. Often overlooked

ARVN troops in Quang Tri Province in the far north of the country were quickly overwhelmed by the North Vietnamese onslaught.

too was the essential role of Air Force and Army airborne forward air controllers in identifying and marking targets and coordinating airstrikes. These small, low-flying aircraft were highly vulnerable and seven were lost to ground fire or SA-7s by mid-May.[28]

Although months more of hard fighting still lay ahead and the battlefield situation remained precarious, the North Vietnamese offensive clearly had been blunted and with it Hanoi's best chance of militarily altering the political dynamic in Paris. Thanks to the overwhelming air response, the North had paid dearly in losses of men and equipment and Saigon's battered and demoralized forces had gained desperately needed breathing space to prepare for the next round. The battle, however, was far from over. Much more still needed to be done. It would come in the form of Operation Linebacker and the air war returning to the skies over North Vietnam with a vengeance. Now it was the Americans' turn to turn the tables.

An American adviser looks on as South Vietnamese officers attempt to grapple with the unfolding offensive. Unlike the 1968 Tet Offensive no U.S. ground troops would be coming to the rescue.

Between April 18 and May 3, three of the big C-130 transports would be lost to enemy ground fire while resupplying the embattled garrison at An Loc. (Photo National Museum of the U.S. Air Force)

3. AMERICAN AIR POWER HEADS NORTH

In retrospect the Easter Offensive or something similar was bound to happen as both Hanoi and Washington pursued likeminded political-military strategies that placed them on a collision course. And while both rationally recognized that victory on the battlefield was beyond their grasp by 1972, each was still more than willing to give it one more try in the faint hope of delivering a coup de grâce. Thus, in one decisive stroke the war could be ended; no more dilly dallying in Paris. Both sides would come close to seeing these hopes fulfilled, but events beyond either's control would conspire—as they often do in war—to snatch seeming battlefield victory from their hands at the last moment.

Setting the Stage

Hanoi's opening gambit in the early days of the Easter Offensive surely looked like a winner. Saigon's forces had taken a beating and given up considerable ground in the north of the country. Key government garrison towns in the south and the central highlands were soon cut off and besieged. American and South Vietnamese air power had staved off immediate defeat and bought time for Saigon, but how long they could maintain the effort was open to question. Moreover, with a paltry 95,000 Americans in country (nearly a quarter of which were Air Force personnel) there would be no U.S. ground combat units rushing to the rescue as they had done in 1968.[1] The Thieu government was in serious trouble. Hanoi knew it and so did Washington.

While Nixon's phased troop withdrawal from Vietnam was politically calculated to undercut his most vehement anti-war critics at home and allow time for full Vietnamization of the war, it also inevitably put Washington in a highly vulnerable

Hastily organized South Vietnamese airborne troops attempt a relief of An Loc in early April 1972.

Hanoi deployed mobile anti-aircraft weapons, such as the 57-mm ZSU-57-2 (pictured), as well as 37-mm towed anti-aircraft guns and man-portable SA-7 surface-to-air missiles to South Vietnam for the first time during the Easter Offensive to counter low-flying American and South Vietnamese aircraft. (Photo National Museum of the U.S. Air Force)

military position and steadily weakened its negotiating leverage with Hanoi. Nixon's military advisers had been deeply concerned that the approach would embolden the North once a theoretical crossover point was reached, whereby the United States would be too weak to respond effectively to Hanoi's military provocations. Kissinger, for his part, saw it as undermining his ability to link American drawdowns to comparative North Vietnamese troop reductions in South Vietnam as a quid pro quo at the Paris talks. The launching of the Easter Offensive seemed to confirm these worse fears. During an early May meeting in Paris the North Vietnamese delegation refused to discuss a ceasefire and Le Duc Tho expressed his growing confidence that "the prospects for the North Vietnamese were looking good,"[2] given the situation on the ground in South Vietnam.

This confidence, which surely reflected the popular view in Hanoi too, while well-founded given the early success of North Vietnamese forces, overlooked or downplayed several critical factors that would ultimately prove to be the North's undoing and turn the tide of battle against it.

First, the ability of the North to mass more than 200,000 men along with tanks and heavy artillery for an offensive along three independent axes was indeed an impressive feat. Even more so that the preparations and staging of forces were accomplished in the face of persistent American and South Vietnamese interdiction efforts. While the initial weight of the onslaught quickly sent the South Vietnamese defenders reeling, Hanoi seriously underestimated the effort it would take to keep its forces supplied and reequipped for any extended campaign, especially as their lines of communication grew increasingly longer and susceptible to air attack.

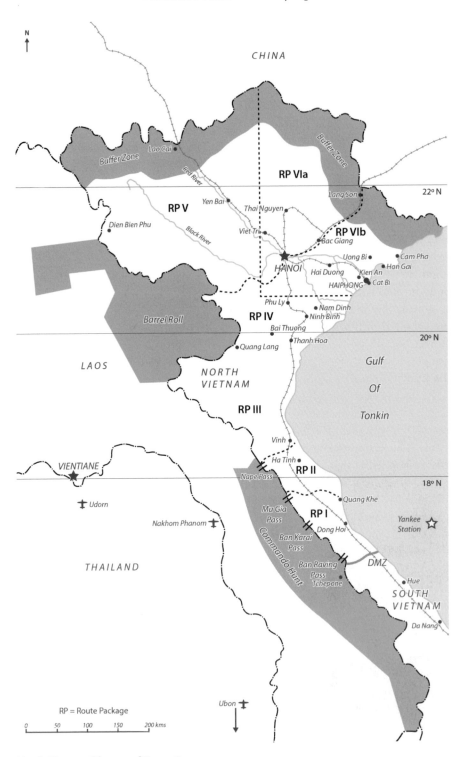

North Vietnam Theater of Operations, 1972.

Second, the politburo's decision to move away from a protracted guerilla warfare strategy by building a more conventional force structure aligned well with its belief that Vietnamization was foundering. Thus, it followed that Saigon's forces would be unable to withstand the North's might when locked into a conventional war. All this came at a cost, however, as the North Vietnamese were now increasingly dependent on the Soviet military pipeline to maintain this conventional force structure. Likewise, this new Soviet dependence and war strategy irritated the Chinese, who saw it as further indication of their waning political and military influence with Hanoi. Although Washington's diplomatic efforts to drive a wedge between Hanoi and its key communist allies had yet to yield fruit, the potential consequences of American success also put the North's new war strategy on dangerous footing.

Lastly, Hanoi not only underestimated the quickness and effectiveness of the American military reaction to their offensive, but also was overconfident in its ability to cope with the reaction. It terribly misread Nixon the man, the cold calculating politician who was willing to do whatever it took to ensure his legacy of bringing America peace with honor in Vietnam. And while certainly true that American military strength in Vietnam was at an all-time low in the spring of 1972 and had adopted a defensive and supporting posture, the U.S military presence in Southeast Asia still remained quite formidable. Air power topped the list. At the start of the year the United States still maintained a force of 385 aircraft (less than one-third strike) in South Vietnam and another 448 (nearly half of them strike) at bases in Thailand,[3] while Navy aircraft carriers operating

Knocked-out and captured North Vietnamese T-54/55 tank in the aftermath of the battle for An Loc.

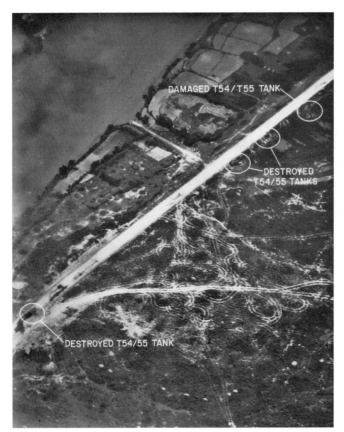

Destroyed and damaged North Vietnamese T-54/55 main battle tanks litter a road near Dong Ha in Quang Tri Province following an airstrike on April 12, 1972. When weather conditions permitted South Vietnamese and American strike aircraft and gunships pounded attacking enemy columns mercilessly.

in the Gulf of Tonkin added an additional 200 aircraft to the total.[4] It would be these air assets and their reinforcements that would be called upon to deliver Washington's initial response to the North's invasion. Ironically, because Nixon had few available options he was more than willing to engage in brinkmanship by pushing the limits of American air power. Or as Nixon bluntly put it, "The bastards have never been bombed like they're going to be bombed this time."[5]

The most pressing need was to beef up American air assets in Southeast Asia as quickly as possible. First to arrive in Da Nang, South Vietnam, in early April were U.S. Marine F-4 squadrons, VMFA-115 and VMFA-212 from Japan, along with the Air Force Phantoms of the 35th Tactical Fighter Squadron (TFS) out of Korea.[6] The majority of additional planes, however, would come directly from U.S. Air Force bases in the United States under Operation Constant Guard that began on April 11. In less than five days three Air Force Phantom squadrons along with all their men and equipment were able to deploy from the United States to Thailand and were soon flying combat missions. Another 108 F-4s, two squadrons of C-130 transports, 16 KC-135 tankers, and nearly 100 additional B-52 heavy bombers would also soon arrive in theater.[7] In all the Air Force would send the equivalent of 15 squadrons and 70,000 men to Southeast Asia in the opening months of the Easter Offensive, while the

South Vietnamese and American artillery batteries fired off tens of thousands of high-explosive rounds in an attempt to stem the enemy advance.

Navy would increase its air order of battle to an unprecedented six carrier air wings with more than 500 aircraft by May.[8] In short order, the number of available American strike aircraft had more than doubled.

Although still precarious after more than a month of fighting, the situation on the all three South Vietnamese battlefronts had slowly begun to stabilize by early May. Saigon and its military had apparently weathered the worst of the storm. Now it was time for the Americans to turn the tables on Hanoi. Accordingly, U.S. air commanders began gearing up for the largest aerial offensive since the end of Operation Rolling Thunder, one that pulled no punches and was designed to finally bring the war to an end.

The Opening Act—Freedom Train

Even as the chaotic struggle in South Vietnam continued to play out, a new American bombing campaign against North Vietnam got underway on April 6. Codenamed Operation Freedom Train, the new effort targeted Hanoi's supply lines, lines of communication, logistics facilities, and supporting military infrastructure from the DMZ northward to the 20th parallel to impede the vital southern flow of reinforcements, equipment, and supplies needed to maintain the momentum of the Easter Offensive. American tactical airstrikes and resupply missions in support of embattled South Vietnamese

General John Vogt, commander of the Seventh Air Force, during the height of the 1972 air campaign.

The Marine base and airfield at Da Nang in the far north of the country once again became a central hub for supporting air operations both in South Vietnam and north of the DMZ following the start of the Easter Offensive.

troops were still the number one priority, but U.S. air commanders dedicated considerable assets to Freedom Train operations as Nixon urged the newly appointed Seventh Air Force commander, General John Vogt, to be both "aggressive and imaginative" in his approach,[9] the irony of which was probably not lost on Vogt, who was replacing a man in General John Lavelle whose aggressiveness and imaginative approach to bombing North Vietnam in the past had cost him his job.

The first airstrikes focused on attacking key logistics and transportation centers supporting the enemy offensive at Vinh and Dong Hoi, as well as against rail and road traffic along Highway 1. This would not be an easy task given the time Hanoi had to prepare and its greatly augmented air defenses throughout the southern panhandle. But the Americans had upped their game too. On April 9 a formation of 12 B-52 Stratofortresses supported by dozens of Air Force and Navy aircraft struck the railyard and an underground POL storage facility at Vinh in the first use of the heavy bombers over North Vietnam since October 1968.[10] Following up this attack three days later, 18 U-Tapao-based B-52s struck the MiG airfield at Bai Thuong, about 25 miles west northwest of Thanh Hoa. One MiG-17 was destroyed on the ground and the runway was heavily cratered.[11] On April 21 and 23, more bomber missions were launched against warehouse complexes near Thanh Hoa that involved 36 Stratofortresses out of U-Tapao air base, Thailand; one bomber was heavily damaged by

Air Force F-4 Phantom squadrons at Ubon and Udorn air bases in Thailand would be stretched to the limit supporting air operations in both North and South Vietnam over the course of 1972.

an SA-2 missile during the April 23 attack and forced to divert to Da Nang for an emergency landing.[12] Before the end of the month American pilots achieved a major psychological victory too. On April 27 Air Force F-4s from the 8th Tactical Fighter Wing (TFW) out of Ubon air base, Thailand used five 2,000-pound electro-optically guided bombs, or EOGBs, to collapse part of the western span of the Thanh Hoa bridge—the infamous Dragon's Jaw bridge that had defied Rolling Thunder attacks for more than three years—and close it to traffic.[13]

Hanoi responded by forward-deploying MiG-21 fighters to Bai Thuong airfield in late April in the hopes of intercepting future B-52 raids and scoring a major victory by downing one of the big bombers. This resulted in Navy A-6 Intruders and A-7 Corsairs off the USS *Coral Sea* and USS *Kitty Hawk* targeting the airfield on several occasions and during a May 6 strike VPAF pilots rose to challenge the American attackers. In what would presage events to come, Navy F-4 Phantoms were able to shoot down two MiG-21s and one MiG-17 with Sidewinder air-to-air missiles that day.[14] Following this setback, the MiGs at Bai Thuong were withdrawn to more protected bases around Hanoi.

In addition to these targeted strikes, Air Force and Navy aircraft patrolled the skies on armed reconnaissance missions ("armed recces") south of the 20th parallel seeking out and attacking truck convoys, coastal and riverine watercraft, and ferreting out hidden supply depots and storage facilities.

While much of this new air offensive mimicked previous tactics and objectives of Rolling Thunder, the air threat in Route Package I—the operational area north of the DMZ up to Quang Khe—had risen enormously. Dozens of deadly SA-2 surface-to-air missile batteries were now deployed there, not only around important targets, but also right up to the DMZ to directly threaten allied air operations in the northern provinces of South Vietnam. Highlighting this danger, a U-Tapao-based B-52D flying an Arc Light bombing mission near Quang Tri on April 8 was seriously damaged by shrapnel from a missile explosion and was forced to make an emergency landing at Da Nang.[15] Air Force efforts to take out these SAM sites met with mixed success and cost them several aircraft.

The Navy also lost at least four planes to SA-2 missiles in the first four weeks of Freedom Train while attacking targets in the Dong Hoi area.[16]

Somewhat surprisingly given Nixon's bellicose attitude, the new air effort against the North was off to a rather restrained start. So far nothing north of the 20th parallel in the North Vietnamese heartland was being bombed. This reflected a divided White House. Kissinger was deeply worried that any American bombing of the Hanoi-Haiphong area might not only jeopardize the Paris peace process, but could also cripple détente with the Soviet Union and the scheduled Strategic Arms Limitation Talks (SALT) summit in Moscow between President Nixon and General Secretary Leonid Brezhnev in May. Secretary of Defense Laird was also unenthusiastic, worried that an escalation might provoke Congress into slashing war funding at a critical time. However, others like deputy national security adviser Alexander Haig and members of the Joint Chiefs, wanted to send a strong message to Hanoi to stand down its offensive or else suffer the consequences. A compromise was reached in the form of Operation Freedom Porch Bravo, a limited one-day attack "against key logistics targets in the Haiphong and Hanoi complexes."[17]

In the predawn hours of April 16 a formation of 17 B-52s from 307th Strategic Wing (SW) flying overnight from U-Tapao rained down some 460 tons of bombs from 34,000 feet on Haiphong's main POL storage facility, igniting intense fires and triggering secondary explosions. Preceding the attack 15 Navy A-6 Intruders struck various SAM sites around Haiphong, while 20 Air Force F-4s laid a corridor of chaff—tens of thousands of small stripes of aluminum to confuse enemy radars and guidance systems—to screen the bombers as still other aircraft provided MiG combat air patrol and electronic

Andersen Air Force Base on Guam—"the Rock of the Pacific"—would become a major staging point for the B-52 bomber build-up as part of Operation Bullet Shot beginning in February 1972 and eventually would be home to nearly 150 B-52s. (Photo National Archives)

With an ability to lay waste to a 1.5-mile-long by half-mile-wide area, B-52 Arc Light bombing missions were extremely effective in breaking up massed troop formations and devastating attacking enemy forces. (Photo National Museum of the U.S. Air Force)

countermeasure (ECM) support.[18] As daylight broke over Haiphong a thick column of bellowing smoke could be seen by the sailors aboard the *Kitty Hawk* more than a hundred miles out to sea.[19] A post-strike damage photo assessment indicated that 17 POL storage tanks, along with several nearby warehouses, railroad tracks, and 30 pieces of rolling stock had been destroyed in the attack.[20]

A second and third wave of close to 100 American aircraft soon followed during the day with strikes by Air Force F-4s and Navy A-7s on ten other targets. Hanoi's main POL storage facility outside the city was hit by a 32-plane F-4 strike,[21] while A-7s bombed Haiphong's Cat Bi and Kien An airfields along with several warehouse and storage complexes in the Haiphong area. As expected, the strikes encountered heavy anti-aircraft fire and more than 250 surface-to-air missiles were fired, although most in a haphazard manner indicating the effectiveness of American countermeasures. Reacting MiGs of the 921st Fighter Regiment engaged Air Force F-4s near Hanoi, but ended up on the losing end; pilots with the 432nd Tactical Reconnaissance Wing (TRW) out of Udorn air base shot down three MiG-21s in aerial combat and a fourth crash while attempting to land. The Navy also destroyed three MiG-17s on the ground a Kien An.[22] U.S losses for the entire operation were an Air Force F-105G Wild Weasel and a Navy A-7E downed by SA-2 missiles.[23]

The raids were deemed highly successful in both sending a message of American resolve and in destroying about half of the North's POL storage and large amounts of stockpiled war supplies.[24] Soviet reaction to the strike was surprisingly muted and SALT summit preparations continued to move forward. Nixon was pleased too, remarking to one of his advisers that "we really left them our calling card this weekend."[25]

B-52D returns home to U-Tapao air base, Thailand, following a mission.

Nonetheless, neither the attacks on Hanoi-Haiphong nor the ongoing bombing south of the 20th parallel did little to change the minds of the North Vietnamese leadership in light of their successes on the South Vietnamese battlefield. Quang Tri city had fallen on May 1. An Loc was under siege and attacks in the central highlands against Kontum and Pleiku were still gaining momentum. With Hanoi feeling its oats and General Abrams reporting from Saigon that "it is quite possible that the South Vietnamese have lost the will to fight,"[26] Nixon had little choice but to up the ante and unleash the full might of American air power against the North. Escalating the war at this point was a huge political and military gamble, but one Nixon felt he had little choice. The war needed to be settled and if Hanoi wouldn't do that in Paris, then Washington would try to do it on the battlefield.

Upping the Ante

A key to stopping Hanoi's offensive in the South lay in the ability of the United States to significantly slow the flow of men, equipment, and supplies to the battlefield, but past American air interdiction campaigns had been only marginally successful and the current Freedom Train operations alone were unlikely to produce the desired unless something dramatically different was done.

American military planners had long recognized the limitations of strategic interdiction as long as the North Vietnamese had an open-ended and uninterrupted source of supply from outside the country.[27] In particular, Hanoi's war machine was heavily dependent on resupply by sea. According to U.S. intelligence estimates, nearly 85 percent of the North's imports—including practically all its oil shipments—came by sea, mainly from the Soviet Union and Eastern Europe.[28] Moreover, virtually all of Hanoi's sophisticated military equipment from surface-to-air missiles, fighter aircraft, and air defense equipment to tanks and heavy artillery flowed through Haiphong's

In response to the Easter Offensive the Navy would increase its presence in the Gulf of Tonkin by May 1972 to an unprecedented six carrier air wings comprising upward of 500 aircraft. (Photo Naval History and Heritage Command)

docks, making the port a critical chokepoint. Accordingly, a blockade of Haiphong and of other smaller North Vietnamese ports through the sowing of minefields would likely have a profound impact on the North's ability to prosecute the war. It would also clearly signal Washington's willingness to escalate the conflict if need be.

While militarily sound, a mining blockade of North Vietnamese ports was risky. "Neutral" communist-flagged ships would be put in direct danger and the mining could precipitate serious diplomatic blowback and at a time when Washington was seeking improved relations with Moscow, as well as the Kremlin's help in advancing the Paris peace talks. It might also backfire and spur increased Chinese military aid to Hanoi to counter the American blockade. Nonetheless, Nixon bit the bullet. Relying on his firm determination to ensure American international credibility in a post-Vietnam world and to seize the opportunity to turn the tide of the war, Nixon authorized the mining on May 5 and the launching of a full-scale air assault against the North, in what Kissinger would later call "the finest moment of Nixon's Presidency."[29]

On the morning of May 8 six Navy A-7s and three Marine A-6s launched from the deck of the *Coral Sea* carrying at total of 36 MK-52 1,000-pound electromagnetic mines to sow the first minefield in the main shipping channel into Haiphong. Operation Pocket Money was underway. The plan called for a quick run-in with all nine aircraft dropping their mines in a single pass to avoid the anticipated heavy anti-aircraft fire from shore batteries. To maintain the element of surprise other Navy planes launched diversionary strikes away from Haiphong, while ECM jammers and fighter escorts screened the attack force. Two guided-missile cruisers, the USS *Chicago* and USS *Long Beach*, were also moved into position off the coast to provide radar warning coverage and defensive missile fire should North Vietnamese fighters react. Despite all these preparations, it would be a tricky

Above: F-4J Phantoms of VF-92 (foreground) and an A-7E Corsair II from VA-146 aboard the USS *Constellation* in May 1972 prior to the onset of Linebacker I. (Photo Naval History and Heritage Command)

Below: An A-7E of VA-22 loaded with MK-52 sea mines on the eve of the mining of Haiphong harbor in May 1972. (Photo U.S. Navy)

A Marine A-6 from VMA-224 prepares to launch from the deck of the USS *Coral Sea* as part of Operation Pocket Money, the mining of Haiphong harbor on May 8, 1972. (Photo National Archives)

mission that would test the skill and nerve of the pilots, who were all dropping aerial mines in combat for the first time.

Skimming just 50 feet above the water to avoid radar detection and negate the SAM threat, the heavily laden jets made a beeline for the harbor channel shortly before 0900. Suddenly the *Chicago*'s radar picked up four enemy fighters heading southeast from Hanoi toward the strike force. The cruiser quickly fired a salvo of Talos surface-to-air missiles at the enemy formation, downing one MiG and forcing the others to scatter. Meanwhile, the strike force pressed on against light and not very accurate anti-aircraft fire and within the space of a few minutes all 36 mines were in the water without the loss of any aircraft. The mines would self-activate within 72 hours and nine ships took advantage of the warning to depart, but 27 others found themselves trapped in the harbor.[30]

Even before the pilots touched down on the deck of the *Coral Sea*, President Nixon was informing the American public of the mining of Haiphong harbor in a televised address and of his decision to begin a new, intense strategic bombing campaign against North Vietnam. Nixon noted he reluctantly took these actions in response to Hanoi's continuing offensive in South Vietnam and its refusal to negotiate an acceptable settlement to the war. The time for talking was over. The next five months would witness an escalation of the air war that went well beyond any campaign heretofore and, this time, American air commanders were hell bent on getting it right.

Linebacker is Launched

In drawing up the new air offensive against the North, the Chairman of the Joint Chiefs, Admiral Thomas Moorer, sought to build on the momentum of Freedom Train operations to develop a hard-hitting campaign designed to once and for all destroy Hanoi's war making capacity. In short, it was to be American air power unleashed. Linebacker, as the new operation was named, would be a decidedly marked departure from the past: no White House micromanagement, no complex bombing or targeting restrictions. It would be first and foremost a military operation, but one with a single, clear singular political objective of ending the war for the United States.

The bombing campaign began in earnest on May 10 with the first Linebacker missions flown against targets in the Hanoi-Haiphong heartland and, as if to underscore the high stakes involved, that day's events would dramatically signal the start of the most intense and ultimately decisive period of aerial combat of the entire Vietnam War.

The USS *Constellation*'s Carrier Air Wing 9 (CVW-9) opened the campaign with 17 of its A-6s and A-7s attacking Haiphong's main POL storage facility (the same one that had been heavily damage by B-52s during Operation Freedom Porch Bravo) with more than 50 tons of MK-82 500-pound bombs, leaving the facility badly damaged and in flames.[31] The strike was preceded by F-4 flak suppressors and A-7 Iron Hands—SAM suppression

Chairman of the Joint Chiefs, Admiral Thomas Moorer (far left) along with the other Joint Chiefs and Secretary of Defense Laird in January 1973. Admiral Moorer was tasked with developing a strategic interdiction bombing campaign to dramatically cut the flow of men and matériel southward and to curtail Hanoi's war-making capacity by striking at the North's heartland in May 1972. (Photo Department of Defense)

missions—engaging anti-aircraft positions and SA-2 missile batteries. Additional Navy F-4 Phantom fighters provided a combat air patrol screen to the west of the city. Two more waves of some 60 Navy aircraft soon joined in the air assault on Haiphong. The *Constellation's* planes busied themselves with cratering the downtown railyard, while aircraft from the *Kitty Hawk* were able to drop a span of the main highway and rail bridge out of the city.[32] In all the Navy would fly 176 attack sorties that first day of Linebacker without a single aircraft loss; one RA-5 Vigilante aircraft flying a post-strike reconnaissance mission did suffer serious damage from SA-2 missile shrapnel.

Meanwhile in the skies over Hanoi some 55 miles to the west, the Air Force was getting into the act in a big way by sending 117 attack and support aircraft into the fray. The main strike force was composed of 32 F-4 Phantoms from the 8th TFW carrying an array of precision guided and conventional munitions, while 12 F-105G Wild Weasels provided air defense suppression and 28 Phantom fighters from the 432nd TFW out of Udorn, Thailand flew air cover for the strike force.[33] In what would become a familiar routine dozens of other aircraft were tasked with providing ECM, communications, early warning, reconnaissance, rescue, and refueling support for the attack. Their targets for that morning were the

The USS *Constellation* would make her sixth and final combat deployment of the war beginning in October 1971 along with the squadrons of Air Wing 9. The wing's F-4s would score nine air combat victories, including five by the war's first ace, Lieutenant Randall Cunningham. (Photo National Archives)

The Navy's advanced all-weather A-6 Intruder would prove to be highly capable of delivering large payloads against heavily defended North Vietnamese targets both day and night.

Paul Doumer Bridge and the railyard at Yen Vien, just to the east and northeast respectively of downtown Hanoi. As one of the best well-defended cities in the world the attackers would be flying into the belly of the beast.

Knocking out the mile-long Paul Doumer Bridge was a top priority. The mile-long rail and highway bridge spanned the Red River linking downtown Hanoi with its eastern districts and was the city's only rail link to Haiphong, as well as being the only rail crossing of the river for southbound traffic within 30 miles. It had been successfully bombed and disabled by the Air Force during Rolling Thunder in August 1967, but had since been repaired and was once again fully operational. Just as before it was heavily defended; more than a hundred anti-aircraft guns ranging up to 100-mm ringed the bridge, multiple SA-2 missile batteries sites covered the skies above, and three major MiG fighter airfields were within a few minutes' flying time. But in stark contrast to the attack nearly five years before that required some 60 planes and nearly 100 tons of ordnance, this time only 16 F-4s armed with 29 tons of precision guided bombs would be tasked with doing the job.[34]

Preceding the strike groups, eight F-4s released chaff along the flight path, while another eight Phantoms from the 432rd TRW flew combat air patrol to counter the anticipated MiG reaction. In addition, each incoming strike group was accompanied by four F-105G Wild Weasels for SAM and flak suppression and four F-4 fighters providing strike escort duties.[35] Anticipation weighed heavily on the pilots and crews, who were expecting a tough fight on their return to Hanoi. They were not to be disappointed.

By mid-morning Major Robert Lodge and his fighter screen found themselves engaged in a twisting and turning dogfight with at least six North Vietnamese MiG fighters northwest of Hanoi. Initially the Americans got the better of the fight, downing three MiG-21s with Sparrow AIM-7 air-to-air missiles.[36] But then a pair of MiG-19s from the 925th Fighter Regiment out of Yen Bai jumped Lodge, sending his Phantom spiraling out of control in a hail of 30-mm cannon fire. Lodge was killed in the attack, while his weapons system officer Captain Roger Locher ejected and spent an amazing three weeks on the ground evading capture before finally being rescued. Meanwhile, the Paul Doumer strike force pressed on from the south of the city, evading barrages of SA-2 missiles—part of around 100 fired

Above: The single-seat A-7 along with its two-man A-6 counterpart would form the backbone of the Navy's air strike arm force during Linebacker I & II. (Photo Naval History and Heritage Command)

Right: An A-7E from the "Dambusters" of VA-195 unloads its bombs on the Hai Doung bridge east of Hanoi on the opening day of Linebacker I. (Photo Naval History and Heritage Command)

Above: Haiphong's shipyard and warehouse complexes come under Navy air attack on May 17, 1972. (Photo National Archives)

Left: Explosions rock a large POL storage site northwest of Vinh after being struck by aircraft from the USS *Kitty Hawk*. (Photo Naval History and Heritage Command)

that day—as they approached their target. Anti-aircraft fire was less than expected and all 16 F-4s were able to release their loads on target. Even though all four of the 2,000-pound EOGBs missed, the other dozen laser-guided bombs (LGBs) scored hits and were able to severely damage the bridge. The next day General Vogt sent a single flight of four Phantoms armed with 2,000- and 3,000-pound laser-guided bombs to finish the job, successfully dropping three spans of the bridge and rendering it inoperable until the end of the war.[37]

The other target that morning would be the nearby railyard at Yen Vien, which was an important transportation and logistics hub for supplies arriving from China. Sixteen Phantoms from the 8th TFW armed with conventional 500-pound bombs were given that assignment.[38] Hot on the heels of the Paul Doumer strike group, the second group of 16 F-4s and their escorts pressed northward to attack and successfully crater the main railyard at Yen Vien with 36 tons of bombs. Once again the attackers were able to evade enemy surface-to-air missiles and anti-aircraft fire, but a lone MiG-19 was able to ambush and shoot down an F-4E escort as it was leaving the target area. Both the pilot and weapons officer were killed.[39]

The day was far from over however. In the early afternoon, 90 naval aircraft launched an attack against the strategic town of Hai Duong midway between Haiphong and Hanoi. It was home to a major railyard, vital rail and highway bridge crossing, and POL storage facility. Several flights of A-7 Iron Hands struck nearby SAM sites, as other Corsairs and Intruders off the *Constellation* began the assault by unleashing a torrent of MK-82 bombs on the railyard. They were soon followed by a second and third wave from the *Coral Sea* and *Kitty Hawk*. Meanwhile, dozens of F-4s provided flak suppression, served as strike escorts or flew MiG combat air patrol to counter the anticipated enemy fighter threat.

The Navy fighter pilots would not have to wait long and soon the *Chicago*'s combat information center that was responsible for tracking and reporting enemy aircraft movements (call sign "Red Crown") was transmitting a flurry of enemy radar contacts. In short order, nearly two dozen VPAF MiG fighters would be airborne and seeking out the Americans. As CVW-9's CAG, Commander Gus Eggert, grappled with coordinating the strikes on Hai Duong from overhead, the wing's combat air patrol broke to intercept the incoming MiGs. What quickly ensued in the skies east of Hanoi was the largest aerial battle of the war, involving no less than 45 American and North Vietnamese aircraft. When it was all over, seven MiG-17s had been brought down by U.S. missile fire without the loss of a single Navy fighter. Notably, Lieutenant Randall Cunningham and his radar intercept officer Lieutenant (j.g.) William Driscoll of VF-96 would rack up three kills that day, pushing their total to five enemy aircraft and thus become the first aces of the Vietnam War.

The day was not yet done for the Navy and by the late afternoon CVW-9 conducted its third alpha strike of the day against harbor facilities at Hon Gai, some 20 miles northeast of Haiphong, as planes from the *Coral Sea*'s CVW-15 simultaneously struck the rail and highway bridge at the port of Cam Pha farther to the east. Both were lightly defended targets and only two MiGs made a brief appearance before retiring without engaging the attackers. The most noteworthy aspect of these strikes were two wayward MK-82 bombs at Hon Gai hitting and seriously damaging a Soviet ship and killing one of the ship's crew.[40] All planes returned safely to their ships by early evening. This brought an end to the first day of Linebacker with American pilots flying more than 400 sorties against the North Vietnamese heartland, leaving in their wake destroyed or heavily damaged rail and highway bridges, cratered railyards, and smoldering storage facilities. Eleven MiGs had been shot down in aerial combat at the cost of two Air Force F-4s; two other Navy Phantoms were lost to SA-2 and anti-aircraft fire and a third was so severely damaged that it was written off.[41]

Above: An A-7E from VA-147 catching the wire aboard the USS *Constellation* after successfully completing its mission. (Photo Naval History and Heritage Command)

Below: Lieutenant Randell Cunningham (left) and Lieutenant (junior grade) William Driscoll (right) of May 10, 1972 fame hold replica F-4 Phantom models as Secretary of the Navy John Warner and Chief of Naval Operations Elmo Zumwalt look on. (Photo Naval History and Heritage Command)

The Emergence of Smart Bombs

Improving the accuracy of aerial bombing has been a constant quest since aircraft were first equipped with bombs. Through advances in technology, bomb design, and pilot training the overall level of bombing accuracy as calculated by circular error probable or CEP—the area described by a circle with the target at its center within which 50 percent of the bombs dropped will fall—had steadily improved from 1,000 feet by the end of World War II to 420 feet at the start of the Vietnam War. For real precision bombing, however, this was not good enough. The bombing of North Vietnam during Rolling Thunder underscored the American need for vastly improved weapons accuracy against well-defended fixed targets, such as bridges, power plants, communications sites, or those high-value targets located close to large civilian populations.

The first smart bomb—actually designated an air-to-ground missile—used in Vietnam was the Navy's AGM-62 "Walleye" in 1967. It was a free-fall munition with a large 825-pound warhead that relied on a television tracking system to lock onto the target. The "fire and forget" Walleyes had some notable successes during Rolling Thunder, particularly their use against Hanoi's downtown thermal power plant in May 1967. Nonetheless, the weapon required a sharp level of contrast to lock onto the target and was often foiled by poor weather. It was also expensive at $35,000 each. The proven concept, however, pushed the Air Force to develop its own electro-optical guide bomb, called Hobo (Homing Bomb System), with improved accuracy and a less costly at $17,000 per copy.

The big breakthrough in smart bombs, however, came with the advent of laser-guided bombs in the late 1960s following a partnership between the Air Force and Texas Instruments to develop a weapon with a maximum CEP of 30 feet. Thanks to the personal efforts of Colonel Joseph Davis, Jr., vice-commander of the Air Proving Ground at Eglin Air Force Base, and Weldon Word, a Texas Instrument engineer, the laser kit concept was born. The kit consisted of a seeker and guidance components that could then be attached to standard conventional bombs and thus, turning them into laser-guided munitions. The specially made seeker head was attached to the nose of the bomb, while the guidance system and control fins were adapted from a Shrike missile and attached to the rear of the bomb. Once released the bomb flew a zigzag course to the target as the fins made corrective adjustments every few seconds to bring the laser reflection back to the center of the seeker head's field of view.

The laser-guide bombs required two airplanes working together. The first acted as the designator to focus a tight laser beam on the target, painting it continuously and reflecting back outward a cone of laser energy called the "basket." The second plane would then drop its bomb into the "basket" allowing the bomb's seeker head to lock onto the laser illumination and home on the target. After successful proof of concept testing at Eglin, a contract was awarded to Texas Instruments in 1967. The Air Force designated the initial version of its laser-guided bombs or LGBs as Paveway.

Combat testing took place in Vietnam in mid-1968 by the 8th TFW at Ubon Air Base in Thailand with good results. The original laser designator device, fabricated by two Air Force officers at Eglin, was mounted on the left canopy rail of the rear cockpit of an F-4 Phantom. It was called the "Zot" by air crews, after the sound effect for the lightning-fast anteater's tongue in the then popular B.C. comic strip. The beam proved sharp and accurate for a distance of more than five miles, but the designator aircraft was required to orbit the target in a left bank of almost 40 degrees at an altitude of 12,000 feet while fixing its beam on the target. Any number of aircraft could then drop their LGBs into the basket. The designator aircraft, however, needed to hold its illumination on the target until the bombs hit (about 30 seconds after release).

While both standard 750-pound MK-117 and 2,000-pound MK-84 bombs were used in combat testing, the more aerodynamic shape of the MK-84 was more amenable to attaching the laser kits and produced an impressive CEP of 20 feet on a consistent basis, with one in every four scoring a direct hit. At 2,000 pounds the MK-84 also produced a much bigger punch and was significantly cheaper—at $3,000 each—than the Walleye and Hobo EGOB options. The end of Rolling Thunder preempted Paveway LGBs use in North Vietnam, but they were used selectively in South Vietnam and Laos over the next four years.

Considerable progress on improving the Paveway system and pilot training was made during the bombing hiatus. By 1972 the Zot box was beginning to be replaced by the Pave Knife laser designator pod. This pod was on a gimbal which swiveled around to keep the laser beam on target, freeing the designator plane to maneuver at will and reduce its vulnerability. Furthermore, the plane could now also drop bombs as well as illuminate the target.

At the time of the 1972 Easter Offensive the Air Force, however, had only seven F-4s equipped with Pave Knife pods so it had to carefully husband this resource. LGBs were used judiciously against the most important and sensitive targets, with Pave Knife being a necessity for the high-threat environment around Hanoi and Haiphong. LGBs produced impressive results. From February 1972 to February 1973, the Air Force dropped more than 10,500 LGBs, resulting in 5,100 direct hits and another 4,000 had a CEP of 25 feet. A later study found that LGBs in Vietnam were "100 to 200 times as effective as conventional bombs against very hard targets." The era of the smart bomb was well on its way.

Source: Adapted from "The Emergence of Smart Bombs," *Air Force Magazine*, March 2010.

The remaining weeks of May saw the air campaign steadily gain momentum and intensify as the Americans stepped up their interdiction efforts against the North Vietnamese transportation and logistics network in the face of dogged resistance by the North's defenders.

Air Force F-4s refueling on their way north. Phantoms operating from bases in Thailand would play a major strike role during Linebacker I, delivering both conventional and laser-guided bombs.

The critically important Paul Doumer Bridge over the Red River east of downtown Hanoi fell under the weight of Air Force laser-guide bombs in the opening days of the air campaign and would remain out of service until the end of the war. (Photo National Museum of the U.S. Air Force)

By mid-month Pocket Money operations had successfully sowed additional minefields of primarily MK-36 DST 500-pound magnetic mines outside the smaller ports Cam Pha and Hon Gai north of Haiphong, as well as in the important river estuaries down the coast at Thanh Hoa, Vinh, Quang Khe, and Dong Hoi. This forced the North Vietnamese into the time- and labor-consuming process of unloading ships into shallow draft boats or barges, thus increasing the unloading time for a 5,000–6,000-ton ship to more than a month[42] and making the small boats and barges vulnerable to attack by U.S. aircraft. This effectively cut the movement of supplies by sea (most notably Soviet oil imports) into the country and made the North increasingly dependent on land routes from China. More than 11,000 mines would eventually be sowed by Navy pilots over the remainder of the year to keep the fields active by periodic reseeding.[43]

As with Rolling Thunder major rail and highway bridges were high-priority targets for Linebacker missions. Those bridges serving as conduits for military equipment and supplies flowing southward from Hanoi and those at key points along the rail and road links to China topped the list. On May 13, the Air Force returned to finish off the infamous Dragon's Jaw bridge at Thanh Hoa that it knocked out of service in late April. This time 14 F-4s from the 8th TFW armed with 2,000- and 3,000-pound LGBs, as well as conventional MK-82s unleashed almost 69 tons of ordnance on the bridge, quickly sending the entire western span into the Song Ma River.[44] Periodic attacks throughout the remainder of the year prevented its repair and kept it out of service until the end of the war. Likewise, several more

An F-105G Wild Weasel armed with two AGM-45 Shrikes on each wing and one AGM-78 Standard ARM (left wing); wing fuel tank on right used to balance AGM-78; QRC-380 jamming blisters on fuselage. The Wild Weasels played an essential role in suppressing North Vietnamese air defenses and thus allowed following strike aircraft a clear pathway to their targets, earning them the motto of "First in, last out." (Photo National Museum of the U.S. Air Force)

EB-66 jammers from the 42nd Tactical Electronic Warfare Squadron at Korat comprised a vital part of Air Force strike packages by seeking to neutralize the North Vietnamese surface-to-air threat. (Photo National Museum of the U.S. Air Force)

key rail and highway bridges along Highway 1 from Vinh southward were also knocked out by Navy strikes in the opening weeks of the campaign.

Meanwhile, in the far north, Air Force laser-guided bombs soon destroyed 13 rail bridges along the northeast and northwest rail corridors that linked Hanoi to the Chinese border.[45] Several bridges, such as the important Lan Giai rail bridge along the northeast line, located inside the 30 nautical mile Chinese buffer zone were struck for the first time in the war. On May 25, 20 F-4s from the 8th TFW bombed the Lan Giai bridge, successfully dropping six of its eleven spans using LGBs and EOGBs.[46] Navy Intruders and Corsairs were also able to disable four other rail bridges between Haiphong and Hanoi during the month as well.

So far Linebacker was off to a good start for the Americans with the Air Force and Navy flying over 6,000 sorties in May. Many key targets had been successfully struck, new countermeasures, precision-guided munitions, and tactics appeared to be working well, 27 VPAF MiGs had been shot down in combat, and the strategic interdiction effort was already beginning to have an impact on Hanoi's offensive in the South. This did, however, come at a cost—20 U.S. aircraft (eleven Navy and nine Air Force) were lost, nine pilots and crewmen were killed, and another 12 were captured.[47] And while undoubtedly pleased with the initial success of the campaign, air commanders and pilots alike knew tough times were still to come, because Hanoi was not about to capitulate without a fierce fight.

4. TURNING THE TIDE

Although certainly not unexpected by any means, the pace and intensity of the new American air assault undoubtedly surprised the North Vietnamese and was a far cry from what they had experienced before. The level of escalation that had taken months or even years to reach in the past was now being accomplished in mere weeks. Not only had the sheer size and scope of the campaign been greater than anticipated, but the U.S. airstrikes were more precise and destructive than ever. Clearly the Americans meant business.

Nonetheless, the North had adapted and weathered American bombing offensives in the past, so Hanoi remained confident of its ability to persevere once again. And although its offensive in the South had been slowed as a result of American air power rushing to the aid of the Saigon regime, Hanoi's forces still were continuing to press the beleaguered South Vietnamese defenders. It would all come down to which side could outlast the other—or which would blink first. The final half of 1972 was quickly shaping up to be a turning point in the war.

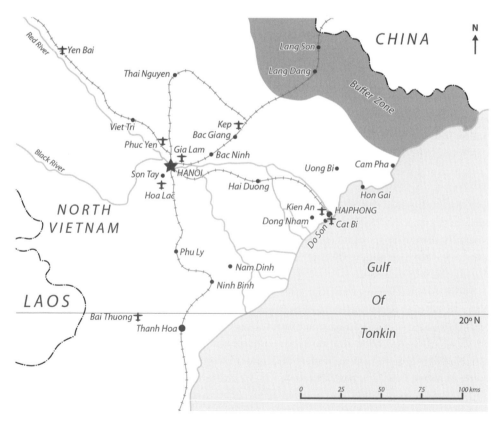

The North Vietnamese Heartland.

Hanoi Girds its Defenses

The North Vietnamese defenders hadn't been sitting idly by during the three-and-half-year bombing hiatus, but had worked feverishly to expand and improve their air defense network and defense capability. As noted earlier, Hanoi had done much by 1972 to augment its defenses in the southern panhandle in the run-up to the Easter Offensive by deploying SA-2 missile batteries right up to the DMZ and along the Laotian border, massing anti-aircraft weapons near major logistics and transportation hubs, expanding its radar coverage, and establishing or improving airfields south of the 20th parallel. Nonetheless, its central focus and the bulk of its defensive resources were still committed to protecting the country's strategic and industrial heartland around Hanoi and Haiphong. As it was here that the North Vietnamese knew the Americans would come calling.

In the early years of the air war over the North the centerpiece of its defenses was the anti-aircraft gun. The more guns the better. Nearly anything that could fire was pressed into service and by the end of the 1966 it was estimated there were upwards of 7,000 weapons from 12.7 mm to 85 mm deployed in an air defense role. Not surprisingly, this curtain of anti-aircraft fire took a deadly toll on the attackers, accounting for approximately two-thirds of all American aircraft losses during Rolling Thunder.[1] By the start of Linebacker, however, improved intelligence collection and attrition indicated that the North's air defense arsenal had declined to about 4,000 weapons and fewer than 1,000 of these were 37 mm or greater.[2]

Once a central component of the North Vietnamese air defense system, anti-aircraft weapons were notably less effective during the 1972 bombing campaign as a result of improved American bombing tactics and the use of precision-guided munitions.

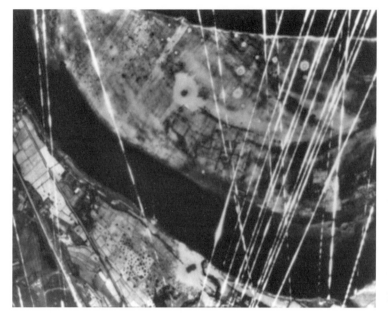

The North Vietnamese continued to ring high-value targets with masses of anti-aircraft guns capable of producing streams of defensive fire to discourage American low-level bombing efforts.

Despite this overall reduction, the most important targets in the Hanoi-Haiphong region remained heavily protected by multiple anti-aircraft positions.

Likewise, the expansion of the North's surface-to-air missile coverage to the entire country by 1972 vastly increased the threat environment for American aircraft, but the bulk of them were concentrated in the Hanoi region as part of 361st Air Defense Division with ten missile battalions defending Hanoi and four more battalions protecting Haiphong.[3] It was believed that the North Vietnamese could field "perhaps 240 SA-2 launchers" rotating across some 300 preprepared sites and post-war analysis indicated that the inventory of SA-2 missiles was likely in excess of 4,000.[4]

The Soviet SA-2 surface-to-air missiles came into service in the Soviet Union in the 1950s and were roughly 35 feet long—giving them the moniker of "flying telephone poles" by American pilots. With an effective range of 25–31 miles and a ceiling of nearly 60,000 feet, they presented a substantial threat to U.S. pilots and crews.[5] Powered by a two-stage solid rocket fuel system, each missile carried a 350-pound warhead of high explosive that could be fused either by contact, proximity or command detonation. A warhead detonating within 200 feet of an aircraft was usually lethal.

A typical North Vietnamese SAM site consisted of four to six launchers laid out in a star-shaped pattern with a central command van, Spoon Rest acquisition radar, and other support equipment at the center along with a Fan Song guidance radar located nearby.[6] The batteries were highly mobile and could reportedly be stood up or broken down in as little as four hours. Soviet doctrine adopted by the North Vietnamese called for the missiles to be fired in pairs a few seconds apart with the hope that the first missile would occupy the pilot's full attention allowing the trailing second missile to home in on the target as it sought to evade the first missile.[7]

Above: SA-2 surface-to-air missiles would pose the greatest threat to U.S. aircraft in 1972. The 35-foot-long missiles had an effective range of 25 to 31 miles and could reach altitudes of nearly 60,000 feet. All 15 B-52s lost during Linebacker II would be to SA-2s. (Photo National Museum of the U.S. Air Force)

Right: Classic star-shaped surface-to-air missile site: SA-2 missile launchers positioned around the perimeter and communications and command vans in the center; Fan Song guidance radar would be located just out of view. (Photo National Museum of the U.S. Air Force)

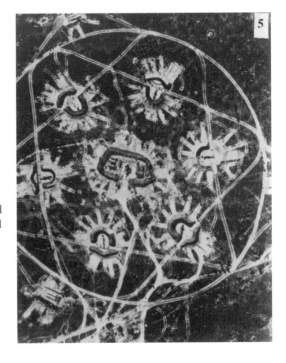

Better training, growing familiarization, and improved equipment also increased the potential lethality of the North's missile system by 1972. New tactics employing decoy sites to mimic the electronic signal of the Fan Song radars were used to confuse pilots or force Iron Hand aircraft to waste their Shrike or Standard ARM anti-radar homing missiles on dummy targets.[8] Likewise, the new capability to optically fire and track SA-2 missiles negated the telltale electronic prelaunch signature, giving U.S. aircraft less warning. An improved SA-2 beacon transmitter was also adopted, which was more difficult for American ECM equipment to jam than the older system.[9] In addition, air defense controllers often attempted to coordinate barrage firings of unguided SA-2s with attacking MiG fighters. The goal of the missile barrage was to distract and harass the American planes into evasive action and thereby allow arriving MiGs to gain a favorable attacking position. The tactic was first used successfully on May 11 to down an F-105G Wild Weasel southwest of Hanoi by MiG-21s.[10]

The largest perceived threat to the American attackers, however, was the vastly strengthened Vietnamese People's Air Force fighter order of battle and the integrated capability of ground control intercept centers to effectively vector MiGs toward U.S. planes. In the spring of 1972 the VPAF could count 246 fighter aircraft in its inventory: 93 MiG-21s—up from 20 during Rolling Thunder—including some advanced models that could be armed with four Atoll air-to-air missiles; 33 highly maneuverable Chinese-made MiG-19s armed with three 30-mm cannons; and 120 older MiG-15s and 17s that comprised the bulk of the VPAF's fighter strength.[11] Age and ongoing maintenance problems, however, usually prevented less than half of these older fighters from being operational at any one time and none of the MiG-15s would see action during Linebacker.[12]

Abandoning vulnerable airfields south of the 20th parallel following the Easter Offensive, as well as those in exposed positions like Kien An and Cat Bi on the outskirts of Haiphong, Hanoi concentrated its four main fighter regiments at bases to the northeast and northwest of the capital. The majority of the MiG-21s were based at Phuc Yen to the northwest of Hanoi, although some occasionally operated out of Yen Bai and Kep too. The 925th Fighter Regiment of MiG-19s operated out of Yen Bai as well as Phuc Yen, while the primary base for MiG-17s was at Kep to the northeast of the capital.[13] Hoa Lac and the international airport at Gia Lam also served frequently as a base for staging fighters too. Accordingly, these airfields (with the exception of Gia Lam) were subject to intense and regular airstrikes from the onset of Linebacker, but never put out of service for any length of time.

Although still far outnumbered by U.S. fighter planes, the VPAF MiGs made the most of their numbers by taking advantage of their early warning radar and ground control network, predictable American tactics, and superior close quarters maneuvering to launch well-timed hit-and-run attacks against strike formations and their supporting aircraft. Ground controllers typically sought to position MiG-21s above and behind enemy aircraft to enable them to make a high-speed approach from the rear to launch their Atoll missiles. Meanwhile the more maneuverable MiG-17s and MiG-19 were positioned to make frontal high-speed passes into the enemy formations from below. In addition, North Vietnamese pilots often played a cat-and-mouse game with their American counterparts in an attempt to lure them into

With the arrival of the A-7D at Korat air base in September and October 1972 the Air Force now had a more capable ground attack aircraft and one with the range to reach all North Vietnamese targets without refueling. (Photo National Museum of the U.S. Air Force)

AC-119 gunships played a major role in interdiction efforts against the Ho Chi Minh Trail in southern Laos and also provided powerful firepower support to embattled ground troops in South Vietnam. (Photo National Museum of the U.S. Air Force)

AC-130 gunships armed with 40-mm cannon and 20-mm mini-guns proved extremely deadly against massed North Vietnamese troop concentrations during the opening months of the Easter Offensive.

An F-4D of the 435th TFS equipped with Paveway II laser-guided bombs (note the seeker head and attached guidance fins). Paveway II was a marked improvement over the more crudely developed Paveway laser-guided bomb kits that were in use during the 1972 bombing campaign. (Photo National Museum of the U.S. Air Force)

F-4Ds of the 435th TFS out of Ubon air base, Thailand heading on a mission to the North in 1972. The versatile Phantom could be configured as an air-to-air fighter, ground attack aircraft or in an air defense suppression role.

F-4 Phantom ground crews in Korat and Ubon, Thailand worked tirelessly to maintain the rigor, pace and demands of air operations in the wake of the Easter Offensive. (Photo National Museum of the U.S. Air Force)

F-111A air crew, who formed part of the 474th TFW that was rushed to Takhli, Thailand in September 1972 to enhance the Air Force's night strike capability. (Photo National Museum of the U.S. Air Force)

The F-111A, here armed with cluster bombs, had an advanced terrain-following navigation system, which enabled it to fly at high speed just above ground level. Its ability to strike quickly and silently, earning it the North Vietnamese nickname of "Whispering Death." (Photo National Museum of the U.S. Air Force)

Above: Captains Jim Boyd and Kim Pepperell from the 17th Wild Weasel squadron landing their F-105G at Korat after completing one of the last Wild Weasel missions of the war on December 29, 1972. (Photo U.S. Air Force)

Right: Flatbed loads of M-117 general-purpose 750-pound bombs await loading on B-52s at Andersen Air Force Base, Guam in 1972. (Photo U.S. Air Force)

F-105G Wild Weasel of the 561st TFS, Detachment 1 and armed with Shrike missiles on the flight line at Korat, Thailand in 1972. (Photo National Museum of the U.S. Air Force)

The specialized EB-66 jammer aircraft and crew played a major role in the electronic countermeasure effort against North Vietnamese air defenses from 1965 to 1973. (Photo National Museum of the U.S. Air Force)

The Navy's advanced A-6 Intruder played a major role in sustaining the American bombing campaign over North Vietnam, because of its ability to deliver 10,000 pounds of ordnance on target under the most adverse weather conditions both day and night. (Photo U.S. Navy)

The A-7E with its groundbreaking computer bombing system was able to deliver half its payload consistently within 90 feet of its target and could also be used in a SAM suppression role as an Iron Hand aircraft. (Photo U.S. Navy)

An F-4B Phantom armed with MK-82 bombs and Sidewinder missiles from VF-111 prepares to launch off the deck of the USS *Coral Sea* during Linebacker I. (Photo Emil Buehler Library National Naval Aviation Museum)

Flying F-4J Phantoms equipped with Sidewinder air-to-air missiles, members of VF-96's "Fighting Falcons" downed eight enemy MiGs between January and May 1972. The three MiG-17s shot down by Lt. Randy Cunningham and Ltjg. Bill Driscoll on May 10 upped their total to five and made them the first aces of the Vietnam War. (Photo U.S. National Archives)

Strike formation of A-7Es from VA-147 off the USS *Constellation* during Linebacker I. (Photo A-7 Corsair II Association)

Following the first months of Linebacker I, the obsolete MiG-17 fighters would become a non-factor in North Vietnamese defense strategy, because of chronic operational and maintenance problems. (Photo National Museum of the U.S. Air Force)

The sophisticated MiG-21 armed with Atoll air-to-air missiles became the backbone of the North Vietnamese air intercept effort in the second half of 1972. (File photo)

Navy fighter pilots had a field day against the older MiG-17s on the opening day of Linebacker I, downing seven of them on May 10, 1972. (Photo National Museum of the U.S. Air Force)

Above: A damaged North Vietnamese T-54/44 tanks lies abandoned on the outskirts of An Loc in May 1972.

Left: The South Vietnamese Air Force, with a heavy reliance on the A-1 Skyraider, played a critical role in halting and then stemming the tide of the North Vietnamese Easter Offensive.

The A-37B Dragonfly aircraft provided vital close air support to embattled South Vietnamese ground forces from April to June 1972. (Photo U.S. Air Force)

Captain Steve Ritchie (left) would become the first Air Force ace on August 28, 1972 when he and his weapons officer Captain Chuck DeBellevue (right) downed a MiG-21. DeBellevue along with Captain Jeffery Feinstein would later become aces in their own right, bringing the number of Air Force aces to three. (Photo National Museum of the U.S. Air Force)

Secretary of State William Rogers signing the Paris peace accords formally ending American military involvement in Vietnam on January 27, 1973. Henry Kissinger sits to Rogers's right. (Photo U.S. National Archives)

American POWs preparing to leave Hanoi in February 1973 as part of Operation Homecoming. (Photo National Museum of the U.S. Air Force)

Navy surface combatants, like the USS *Oklahoma City* with its six-inch guns, provided additional firepower against coastal military installations from the DMZ all the way north to Haiphong. (Photo U.S. Navy)

Close-up of an AGM-45 Shrike missile being inspected with the larger AGM-78 Standard ARM present behind it on an early model F-105G Wild Weasel. (Photo National Museum of the U.S. Air Force)

B-52 "bomb clip" being loaded. The Big Belly B-52D models could carry nearly 30,000-pound payloads of 500- and 750-pound bombs. (Photo U.S. Air Force)

Navy personnel load MK-82 Snakeye bombs. (Photo Naval History and Heritage Command)

The 1,000-pound MK-52 sea bottom mine was used in the initial aerial mining of Haiphong harbor on May 8, 1972. (Photo Naval History and Heritage Command)

Navy ordnance men often found creative ways of sending a message to the enemy. (Photo Naval History and Heritage Command)

a MiG or anti-aircraft gun ambush. Despite the disastrous opening day of the campaign, especially for MiG-17s of the 923rd Fighter Regiment, these fighter tactics proved highly effective early on and by the end of June VPAF pilots had achieved an unprecedented 12:13 loss ratio against their air force counterparts; the first time the U.S. Air Force had been on the losing end of an air-to-air ratio.[14] It was all the more galling given the Navy's 19 victories without a loss over the same period.

Thus, protecting the strike force became the centerpiece of American efforts to counter the North's defenses. While the days of large alpha strikes with wave after wave of attack aircraft rolling onto a target were a thing of the past thanks to the advent of precision-guide munitions and improved bombing efficiency, the high threat environment

Right: Chinese-made MiG-19s of the 925th Fighter Regiment operated out of Yen Bai and Phuc Yen airfields and with their three 30-mm cannons and maneuverability proved to be worthy adversaries in the opening weeks of Linebacker I, downing three Air Force F-4s.

Below: The advanced MiG-21s, armed with up to four Atoll air-to-air missiles, would prove to be the biggest air combat threat to U.S. aircraft throughout the 1972 campaign, although the steady loss of planes and experienced pilots limited their effectiveness in the waning months of the year.

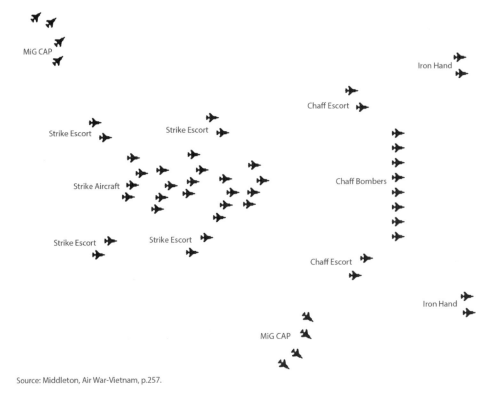

Source: Middleton, Air War-Vietnam, p.257.

Typical Linebacker Strike Force Composition.

over the North Vietnamese heartland required an ever-growing cast of supporting aircraft. It was not uncommon for a typical Air Force Linebacker strike package to consist of a strike flight of eight to 12 F-4s equipped with LGBs and 12 to 16 F-4s armed with conventional ordnance to be supported by upwards of 65 aircraft, including EB-66s jammers providing electronic countermeasures, flights of F-4s laying chaff corridors, teams of F-105Gs Wild Weasels flying SAM and flak suppression, RF-4s providing photo reconnaissance, and dozens of F-4 fighters flying escort and providing combat air patrol.[15] In addition, each mission was assigned a complete complement of aircraft providing search and rescue capability, aerial tanker support, and airborne surveillance and communication capability. Not surprisingly, this level of effort would severely tax both men and air frames throughout the course of the campaign.

Tightening the Screws
The frenetic pace of the campaign on the North continued unabated into the early months of the summer as General Vogt and Admiral John McCain, Jr., as Commander-in-Chief, Pacific Command, sought to maintain the pressure on Hanoi and its ability to continue the offensive in the South, while Nixon and Kissinger hoped that this display of firepower might convince Hanoi to return to the negotiating table.

As a strategic interdiction effort, Linebacker targeted key elements of the North Vietnamese transportation and supply network, as well as critical components of Hanoi's military-industrial infrastructure. A tangential mission requirement called for the degrading of the North's air defenses. In conjunction with Linebacker operations, U.S. aircraft were simultaneously flying tens of thousands of close air support and resupply sorties in support to ARVN troops; more than 13,000 sorties around Hue alone by June.[16] Air operations in South Vietnam, in fact, consumed the majority of the Air Force's workload throughout the Linebacker campaign.

Thanks to the closure of North Vietnamese ports, Hanoi was now entirely dependent on overland routes from China to meet its nearly 150,000 tons per month of imports. The two rail lines and eight major roads out of China, which had previously carried only 15 percent of supply requirements,[17] were now forced to carry the entire burden. It was up to the 8th TFW to close down these routes or at least make resupply as difficult and time consuming as possible. Thanks to the use of precision-guided munitions, General Vogt would be able to claim that "we had 15 bridges out on each railroad at any given time—as fast as they would build them, we would knock them out again."[18] Not only was the bombing effective, but it had become much more efficient—five bridges were destroyed in one day using 24 LGBs, a feat that likely would likely have required more than 2,000 unguided bombs during Rolling Thunder.[19]

The assault on the transportation and supply network extended well beyond the Chinese rail and road corridors, with the Navy assuming much of the burden south and east of the capital and along the rail and road corridor from Thanh Hoa southward all the

The USS *Saratoga* would make its one and only Vietnam deployment in 1972, but it was during the most intense period of combat from May 1972 to January 1973. Its Air Wing 3 would pay a heavy price: 13 aircraft lost in combat and another four in operational accidents. (Photo U.S. Navy)

MiG-21 pilots in Soviet-made high-altitude flight suits. At the beginning of 1972, the best and most experience VPAF pilots flew the MiG-21 interceptors and over the course of the year they would be credited with downing 26 American planes. (Photo National Museum of the U.S. Air Force)

way to Dong Hoi. Typical of this effort was the 33-plane alpha strike launched by the USS *Saratoga's* CVW-3 against the rail and highway bridge over the Song Day River at Phu Ly, about 40 miles south of Hanoi. In the face of heavy anti-aircraft fire, A-7s and A-6s were able to heavily damage both bridges with Walleye EOGBs, as well as destroy an estimated 75 percent of the nearby military storage area with conventional bombs.[20] Continuous strikes by naval aircraft in the Thanh Hoa, Vinh, and the Dong Hoi areas throughout June and July were also effective in hampering North Vietnamese bridge repair efforts.

By the end of June the Air Force alone claimed to have destroyed more than 100 bridges and intelligence analysts estimated that there was no uncut stretch of the North Vietnamese rail system longer than 50 miles, forcing a growing dependence on trucks and other labor intensive transfer methods to bypass bombed-out bridges and chokepoints.[21] Moreover, it was believed that monthly imports had been reduced to just 30,000 tons and critical supplies of POL stocks needed to support the offensive in the South were beginning to run low.[22]

Trucks now began to assume a major role in the North's calculus. U.S. intelligence estimates indicated that the North Vietnamese had more than 20,000 trucks in its inventory in 1972 and Chinese production was more than capable in offsetting any losses.[23] Not surprisingly, early June saw a significant surge in trucks carrying supplies as rail lines and rail bridges were rendered inoperable; at one point rising to 40 trucks per mile along the highway paralleling the northeast rail line from China to Hanoi.[24] While some attempts were made to attack these truck convoys, the old method of armed recces in Route Packs V and VI—the operational areas encompassing Hanoi and Haiphong—was deemed too high risk with marginal reward. Instead General Vogt opted to disrupt the truck traffic by destroying highway bridges, as well as attacking vehicle storage area, truck repair facilities, and supply depots. South of the 20th parallel, however, both the Air Force and Navy continued to fly day and night armed recces in search of trucks and other targets of opportunities. Route Packs I and II also saw widespread bombing of storage depots and lines of communication by B-52s as the in-theater bomber inventory increased and the bombers could be diverted from the battlefield in South Vietnam. They would eventually log 260 sorties in June and average 30 per day over North Vietnam through the end of Linebacker five months later.[25] General Vogt later estimated that the bombing and mining interdiction effort reduced supplies flowing southward to the battlefield by at least 20 percent and that by July the enemy was experiencing acute shortages of fuel, food, and ammunition.[26]

In conjunction with the strategic interdiction campaign, numerous strikes were also launched against important industrial facilities, POL storage sites, and key military installations across the North. Some high-profile targets attacked in the opening months included Hanoi's main electric transformer station, the Thai Nguyen industrial complex, the Bac Giang thermal power plant, the Bac Mai air defense and command center, and Haiphong's POL storage facilities. Yet none was more telling than the June 10 destruction of the North's newest and largest hydroelectric facility at Lang Chi, about 65 miles northwest of Hanoi along the Red River. On that day, 12 Air Force F-4s out of Ubon launched a highly choreographed strike on the facility by first blasting an opening through the plant's concrete roof and then dropping time-delayed laser-guided munitions through the hole to destroy the plant's four turbine generators.[27] All this was accomplished without inflicting any collateral damage to the off-limits dam upon which the power plant rested.

Both Air Force Wild Weasels and Navy Iron Hands made extensive use of the AGM-45 Shrike radar-homing missile to destroy active Fan Song SA-2 guidance radars. (Photo National Museum of the U.S. Air Force)

While precision-guided munitions were a game-changer, the overwhelming majority of the bombing was still conducted using conventional ordnance with guided bombs accounting for only 1 percent of the bombs dropped during the war.[28] A critical shortage of the Pave Knife pods used as laser designators was one of the primary factors—by July the Air Force was down to just five of the pods[29]—in limiting LGB strikes to the most high-value targets in the northeast. Thus, to compensate both the Air Force and Navy relied on conventional strikes to maintain the momentum of the campaign and soon American pilots were flying up to 300 sorties a day from the DMZ up to Haiphong. These efforts came at the cost of 21 U.S. aircraft in June, bringing total Linebacker air losses to forty-one.[30]

None of the early bombing successes, however, could have been accomplished without a determined effort to target, degrade, and defeat the North's air defenses. Although the task was the same that faced U.S. air commanders three and half years earlier, technological advancements, more advanced aircraft and avionics, unit specialization, and a maturation of operational tactics provided the American forces with a distinct advantage. The North Vietnamese, for their part, tried to negate many of these advantages by concentrating their limited resources around Hanoi and constantly adjusting and adopting new defensive tactics to keep the Americans off balance. Ultimately, Nixon's willingness to risk fighting an air war of attrition proved too much for the North to overcome.

In May the primary MiG airfields at Kep, Phuc Yen, and Yen Bai, along with six other air bases, were bombed and their runways cratered;[31] some MiGs were also caught on the ground and destroyed. Past American experience, however, had shown that the North

A KC-135 refuels F-4Es (foreground) of an Air Force hunter-killer team; F-105G Wild Weasels in the background. The 1972 creation of hunter-killer teams allowed the Air Force to not just disable or suppress SAM sites, but to destroy them as well with cluster munitions. (Photo National Museum of the U.S. Air Force)

Vietnamese were able to quickly repair any damage to the runways and it was nearly impossible to render the airfields inoperable for any length of time. In addition, aircraft held in reserve were often hidden in caves or dispersed into makeshift huts that were camouflaged as farmers' houses.[32] The VPAF also frequently rotated regiments or individual planes among its various airfields to further complicate U.S. strike planning. Thus, airstrikes against the airfields amounted to more of a harassing tactic than a realistic attempt to destroy the North's fighter capability. This would happen in the skies over Hanoi and Haiphong. Or so the Americans thought.

The opening day's air combat victories seemed to confirm that belief, despite some nagging concerns given the Air Force's losses. The belief in American air superiority, however, was seriously tested throughout June and July as aggressive MiG-21 pilots and coordinated hit-and-run tactics claimed another 13 Air Force Phantoms, while losing only seven of their own. Navy fighters downed three additional MiGs as well, at the cost of one F-4 during the same two-month period.[33] Understandably, frustration among Air Force fighter pilots was growing and malfunctioning AIM-7 radar-guided air-to-air missiles didn't help the situation either.

The left side of a SA-2 site being blanketed by cluster bombs dropped from F-4E Phantoms as part of a hunter-killer team attack. (Photo National Museum of the U.S. Air Force)

The Air Force moved quickly to address the situation with the Air Force Chief of Staff, General John Ryan, taking a direct role by replacing the Seventh Air Force chief of operations with the veteran Major General Carlos Talbott. Vogt for his part, sought to vastly improve the MiG warning system by establishing a new fusion center, call sign "Teaball," at Nakhon Phanom Air Base in far northeastern Thailand. Still, challenges remained as the system required a radio rely via an orbiting EC-121 that often resulted in delays, forcing Air Force pilots to continue to rely heavily on the Navy's Red Crown warnings. Post-mission debriefs, intelligence, and communication coordination were also improved under Vogt.[34]

Some of the biggest changes, however, took place in enhancing training, pilot specialization, and air-to-air weapons. Foremost, the Air Force established the Red Flag combat exercise program at Nellis Air Force Base to closely mimic the Navy's Top Gun school. The latter's worth was clearly demonstrated when Navy F-8 pilots consistently bested F-4 pilots during aerial combat training exchanges at Udorn.[35] This in turn, however, led to improved combat tactics, including the Air Force's growing adoption of the Navy's two-plane "loose deuce" formation that provided increased flexibility and reaction than the old "fluid four" formation.[36] Increased mission specialization with entire wings concentrating on bombing (8th TFW) or performing combat air patrol or escort duties (432nd TRW, 388th TFW) allowed pilots to gain expertise and experience quickly. Considerable effort was also directed at improving the effectiveness of the AIM-7 Sparrow missile, which only

SA-2 missile in flight (top center) over Kep airfield. Despite the best efforts of American electronic countermeasures, use of chaff corridors and clouds, and reliance on SAM suppression aircraft, the SA-2 threat continued to be a constant menace to attacking planes. (Photo National Museum of the U.S. Air Force)

scored hits 20 percent of the time, that led to development of the "dogfight Sparrow" with a more effective minimum range.[37] Likewise, increased inventories at Udorn and Ubon of F-4Es—with a built-in 20-mm nose cannon—gave pilots another close-in dogfighting weapon. Gunfire would eventually account for the shooting down of five MiGs by the end of Linebacker.[38]

These changes, as well as mounting VPAF losses of experienced pilots and planes in the attrition battle turned the tide in favor of the Americans by August. Over the next three months the kill-to-loss ratio would steadily rise to 4:1 in the Air Force's favor, matching the Rolling Thunder's peak performance.[39] This period would also see the first Air Force ace on August 28 when Captain Richard "Steve" Ritchie scored his fifth MiG kill; he would later be joined by two others, captains Charles DeBellevue and Jeffery Feinstein.

Overcoming the threat posed by North Vietnamese anti-aircraft fire and surface-to-air missiles was also a critical factor to the success of the bombing campaign. The heavy concentration of these ground defenses around Hanoi, Haiphong, and other key targets in the northeast of the country challenged the skill and nerve of American pilots. Anti-aircraft fire proved especially deadly during Rolling Thunder, but the advent of precision-guide munitions and advanced computer bombing and navigation systems in the A-7E (which was able to land half its conventional bombs within 90 feet of the target[40]) not only increased the accuracy of the bombing, but put fewer strike aircraft at risk over the target. The biggest change, however, took place in bombing tactics that now allowed aircraft to release their payloads at greater altitude and distance from the target and thus avoid the curtain of protective anti-aircraft fire. Radar-guided 85-mm and 100-mm guns still had the capability to down even the high-attacking aircraft, but increased and more capable electronic counter-measures, like the introduction of the Navy's new EA-6B Prowler, helped mitigate the threat. Nonetheless, the danger remained ever present and aircraft forced below 10,000 feet exposed themselves to often withering fire; anti-aircraft guns claimed at least 16 American planes in the first three months of Linebacker.[41]

Thus, the increased surface-to-air missile presence with their overlapping fields of fire and the North's extensive radar warning network now became the biggest ground fire threat to American planes. The U.S. solution was twofold: defuse or destroy the threat.

In the first instance, the Americans relied heavily on electronic countermeasures to jam or confuse enemy radars and SA-2 Fan Song guidance radars. These included, airborne ECM platforms supporting strike missions, like the Air Force's old standby EB-66 Destroyer or the Navy's ERA-3B Skywarrior and EA-6 Intruder, to newer technology ALQ jamming pods carried by individual planes. Sometimes, however, the simplest countermeasures were the best: the Air Force made extensive and highly effective use of chaff corridors to mask their strike aircraft when approaching targets. Every countermeasure, however, would elicit an enemy response, such as shifting frequencies or wavelengths, which then needed to be countered as each side sought to negate the other's technology.

Destruction of the offending SAM site was clearly the preferred option by American airmen. It required the use of specialized aircraft, weapons, and tactics, but most of all it required men with nerves of steel who were willing to engage in a deadly electronic game of tag with SA-2 missile batteries. Navy A-6 and A-7 Iron Hands and Air Force F-105G

North Vietnamese civilians and local militia comb through the wreckage of an A-7C flown by Lieutenant (junior grade) Stephen Musselman off the USS *America* on September 10, 1972. Musselman was flying an Iron Hand mission south of Hanoi when his aircraft was shot down by an SA-2 and he was killed.

Wild Weasels were an essential component of strike packages in 1972 and the most effective tool for suppressing SAM sites. The Iron Hand concept had been around since 1965, but it had seen considerable evolution in both terms of equipment and tactics by the time of the Linebacker raids. Although AGM-45 Shrike missiles were still plentiful and widely used, they had been supplemented extensively by the AGM-78 Standard ARM, with its larger warhead and capability to lock on to Fan Song radars from a much greater distance. Unfortunately, the Air Force suffered from chronic shortages of the AGM-78s throughout Linebacker. Improved electronic warning and countermeasure systems in both F-105Gs and A-6s helped to increase their survivability and effectiveness however.

American pilots were also constantly adjusting and tweaking their tactics. One tactic was to loft a Shrike missile blindly over a suspected SAM site and then once the Fan Song radar came up the missile would already be prepositioned and ready to home in immediately. Another adaptation was the Air Force creation of "hunter-killer" teams. This involved two F-105G Wild Weasels working in tandem with two F-4Es to not only destroy the radar with a missile hit, but also to completely pulverize the entire site with MK-20 cluster bombs dropped by the Phantoms. The accompanying F-4s also had the added benefit of protecting the F-105s from any potential MiG attack. By the end of August the hunter-killer teams had proven highly effective at forcing the North Vietnamese to modify their tactics, move their launchers more frequently, and pay more attention to camouflaging their SAM sites.[42]

As a result of these combined passive and active countermeasures, the effectiveness of the North's surface-to-air missile threat was vastly reduced, averaging only one kill per 150 missiles fired.[43] Nonetheless, SA-2 missiles would account for the loss of 24 U.S. aircraft during Linebacker. Six of these aircraft—five Navy A-7 Iron Hands and one Air Force F-105G Wild Weasel—along with four pilots and crew, would be lost in the deadly battle with SAMs.[44]

Hanoi's Setbacks in the South

The summer of 1972 was proving to be a difficult time for Hanoi. Just as the air campaign in the North was gaining momentum the last vestiges of the Easter Offensive were grinding to a halt and Hanoi's forces began to face serious reversals in the South. A last-gasp effort to capture the old imperial city of Hue had failed in June in the face of overwhelming U.S. and South Vietnamese firepower, leaving behind at least 600 North Vietnamese dead and nearly two dozen tanks destroyed.[45] The siege of An Loc west of Saigon had been lifted in mid-June and a relief column with reinforcements and supplies reached the city by the end of the month. North Vietnamese forces had pulled back from Kontum in the central highlands and the highway to the encircled city was now opened. With renewed confidence and aggressiveness, ARVN forces were on the counterattack in Quang Tri Province in the far north, as well as in the central highlands throughout July and August as they sought to recover lost territory. American and South Vietnamese aircraft continued to pummel the withdrawing enemy—including nearly 4,900 Arc Light sorties in July and August alone,[46]—as reports of North Vietnamese supply and ammunition shortages among captured prisoners began to increase.[47]

With the exception of the battle to retake Quang Tri city, which would stretch into mid-September, the fighting across the country largely sputtered to an end with no discernable advantage for either side. Saigon continued to control all major cities and the majority of the countryside, but Hanoi's forces remained ensconced in the northernmost provinces and had expanded their grip on territory abutting the Laotian–Cambodian border. Although Saigon's forces had taken a severe beating, suffering some 30,000 dead and losing huge quantities of equipment, they had held the line at key moments and thus allowed massed American firepower to decimate the attacking North Vietnamese and Viet Cong forces. Some estimates indicate that in excess of 100,000 of the attackers died during the Easter Offensive.[48]

Not only was the military offensive shattered, but Le Duan failed once again to incite a popular uprising against the Saigon government. Moreover, the human and material losses would be difficult to replace in the face of the ongoing American interdiction effort. Some high-ranking North Vietnamese officials believed it would be three to five years before they would be capable of launching another major offensive.[49] Clearly Hanoi's military gamble had failed, but what would be its next step and how would the Americans react to the changed battlefield situation?

Now increasingly confident that the military threat to the Thieu government was contained, the Nixon administration—ever mindful of the upcoming elections in November—moved forward on negotiating an end to the war and drawing down American forces. This despite

Throughout the late summer of 1972, ARVN forces in the Quang Tri Province continued to press their counterattack south of the DMZ with the aid of American air power.

strident objections from field commanders, who were fearful of losing their hard-gained military advantage and were worried about operational complications arising from the further loss of personnel and bases in South Vietnam. Shifting air assets over to Thailand helped to mitigate any potential degradation in Linebacker and South Vietnamese air operations, but it added further political stress to an already shaky U.S.–Thai relationship. Nonetheless, the Pentagon withdrew the last U.S. ground combat troops in South Vietnam in mid-August and shortly afterward announced troop reductions that would bring U.S. force levels to no more than 27,000 by December 1.

Peace talks also resumed in Paris. Kissinger and Tho met on July 19 and then again twice more in August to hammer out a settlement, as both sides now reaffirmed their commitment to ending the war. While steady progress was made, numerous sticking points, such the presence of North Vietnamese troops in the South after an American withdrawal, the future of U.S. military assistance to Saigon, and demands for the removal of Thieu from power, were proving difficult to resolve.[50] Moreover, the talks did not spell an end to the Linebacker campaign. Fearful of repeating President Johnson's mistakes during Rolling Thunder, Nixon continued the bombing of the North to maintain the pressure on Hanoi throughout the negotiations. In point of fact, Hanoi was in for a rude awakening as Nixon would be more than willing to unleash the full might of American air power on the North in the remaining months of the year to achieve the favorable settlement he was seeking.

5. THE ILLUSION OF PEACE

While American and the North Vietnamese delegations talked of peace in Paris that summer, the air war over the North not only continued, but grew even more intense. For while Le Duan and the politburo now opted to pursue a pragmatic diplomatic solution to the war, Nixon and his advisers had yet to abandon their military tool of coercion. It would be a colossal mistake for Washington to give up its prime source of negotiating leverage, and Nixon knew it. In addition, senior military officers argued forcefully that scaling back the air campaign now would undercut their gains; Linebacker had "greater impact in its first four months of operation than Rolling Thunder had in three and half years," according to one Air Force general.[1] Moreover, any bombing halt would permit Hanoi to regroup, rebuild, and resupply its forces. Nixon, now increasingly confident of his reelection and support for his war strategy, didn't need much convincing. The bombing would continue.

Closing the Vice

Eager not to repeat the errors of the past nor lose momentum during peace talks, both the White House and the Joint Chiefs pushed to increase the number of Linebacker attack sorties and put more bombs on target. Three carrier air wings were now ordered to concentrate on bombing the North, half of their strikes to be against targets in Route Pack VI.[2] Despite his commitment to smaller, but highly effective laser-guided bombing missions, General Vogt reluctantly agreed in August to fly at least two mass missions—those involving at least 48 strike aircraft—per day against the northern heartland.[3] The Pave Knife pod shortage and the high requirement for non-strike aircraft supporting laser-guide bombing missions, however, meant a return to using less effective conventional bombing methods to achieve this goal. Poor weather conditions over much of the far north of the country throughout August grounded dozens of missions and forced the Seventh Air Force to rely on the long-range all-weather navigation system or LORAN for radar bombing, which produced questionable results.[4] The Navy with its all-weather-capable A-6s and advanced A-7Es would be tapped to make up much of this shortfall by flying near 5,000 sorties in August—the highest monthly total during Linebacker.[5]

Despite these obstacles, the air campaign pressed forward into September as the repulse of the Easter Offensive freed up of more air assets and newly arriving men and equipment made the American air order of battle stronger than ever. Key military, industrial, and transportation targets in the Hanoi–Haiphong–Nam Dinh triangle and along the northeast and northwest rail lines to China were now under near constant bombardment. Likewise, the disabled Paul Doumer Bridge was the target of a September 10 attack by the 8th TFW. An Air Force strike force effectively avoided Hanoi's defenses and four F-4s armed with laser-guided bombs dropped two additional spans of the bridge into the Red River. All strike aircraft returned safely, but a Navy A-7 Iron Hand off the USS *America* was lost and the pilot killed when it was hit by an SA-2 missile.[6]

The USS *Newport News* fires her 8-inch guns against North Vietnamese coastal targets. The *Newport News* along with other cruisers and destroyers comprised Task Unit 77.1, which aggressively shelled enemy military installations and infrastructure from the DMZ to Haiphong harbor between April and December 1972. (Photo Department of Defense)

No part of the country it seemed was safe from the American onslaught. Daily F-4, A-6, and A-7 strikes targeted North Vietnamese air defenses, communications centers, weapons storage and repair facilities, along with industrial complexes, thermal power plants, POL storage facilities, rail and highway bridges, and railyards throughout the North's heartland. Meanwhile, B-52 bombers pummeled truck parks, ammunition and supply depots, and troop concentrations in the southern panhandle. Dozens of day and night armed recce flights also sought out and struck vehicle convoys, coastal shipping, and other targets of opportunity from Thanh Hoa southward to Dong Hoi. The pressure on Hanoi was clearly building.

With the Air Force focusing its efforts on interdicting the supply routes out of China and attacking high-value targets with laser-guided bombs, Navy aircraft picked up the lion's share of this intensified bombing effort. Over the course of September alone seven different air wings—comprising almost 1,500 aircraft—would be hurled against the North as part of Nixon's effort to break the deadlock in Paris.[7] While the sophisticated A-6 and A-7s and their F-4 escorts carried the burden north of the 20th parallel in the high air-threat environment, the venerable, yet reliable A-4 Skyhawks and F-8 Crusaders flying off the USS *Hancock* (now on its seventh deployment of the war) took to the air once again over the southern panhandle. Here they would join Air Force Phantoms of the 8th TFW to interdict lines of communications and harass the enemy from Vinh to Dong Hoi to the DMZ. All this firepower, however, came at a price—19 American aircraft would be lost in combat over the North and six more to operational accidents during the month; eleven pilots and crew would be killed and another six men taken prisoner.[8]

Naval Gunfire Support to the Air Campaign

While air power was the focus of the 1972 campaign against the North, U.S. Navy surface combatants also provided a valuable contribution to the war effort by attacking and inflicting significant damage on variety of North Vietnamese targets from May to December.

A mere two weeks into the Easter Offensive nine destroyers of the newly created Task Unit 77.1 were already operating north of the DMZ, bombarding everything from bridges and road junctions to radar installations, SAM and anti-aircraft sites, and coastal defense batteries as far north as Vinh. Four destroyers along with the cruiser USS *Oklahoma City* also fired more than 600 rounds against shore emplacements on Haiphong's Do Son peninsula on April 14 in support of the Operation Freedom Porch Bravo air raid on Hanoi and Haiphong. So it came as little surprise that Seventh Fleet headquarters integrated surface combatants into the Linebacker interdiction mission from the onset.

During the course of the first two days of Linebacker I, ships of Task Unit 77.1 bombarded Dong Hoi, Vinh, and twice shelled targets in the Haiphong area with 8-inch gunfire from the cruisers USS *Newport News*, *Oklahoma City*, and *Providence*. By mid-May, Task Unit 77.1 had already expended nearly 42,000 rounds. Ranging up and down the coast from Dong Hoi to Thanh Hoa over the coming months, the destroyers and cruisers continued to regularly strike military installations, POL storage facilities, and worked to impede the flow of men and material southward along Highway 1 by targeting the transportation network. Operations were conducted both day and night and often in coordination with airstrikes.

One of the most daring attacks took place on the night of August 27 against a dozen military installations in and around Haiphong harbor. Coastal defense gun emplacements, SAM sites, ammunition depots, and the airfield at Cat Bi were targeted by a four-ship task force that included the *Newport News* and *Providence*. The *Newport News* and the destroyer USS *Rowan* entered the harbor channel before unleashing gunfire, while the other ships bombarded the Cat Bi targets to the southwest. Shore batteries engaging the Americans were estimated to have fired some 300 rounds of heavy artillery at the attackers, but failed to score any hits. Several North Vietnamese patrol boats attempting to intercept the departing ships were either sunk or damaged by a combination of naval gunfire and air attack.

The destroyer USS *Goldsborough* was not so fortunate on the night of December 19 when it and the USS *Hoel* were attacking targets near Hon Me Island north of Haiphong. After successfully shelling a radar installation and road junction, counter-battery fire scored a direct hit on the aft section of the *Goldsborough* with the resulting explosion and shrapnel killing two crewmen and fatally wounding a third. Six other sailors were also wounded. Damage to the ship, however, was considered light and after repairs she return to duty off South Vietnam.

The September tally included the first combat loss of an F-111 aircraft; the planes had just recently arrived in theater for the first time since their ill-fated rushed deployment in March 1968.[9] The aircraft was one of the first six F-111s deployed to Takhli air base, Thailand, with the 429th TFS and was on its first bombing mission southeast of Yen Bai on the night of September 28 when it and its two-man crew were lost under unknown circumstances.[10] The aircraft may have been shot down, flown into the ground or destroyed by shrapnel from its own exploding bombs dropped at very low altitude, but whatever the cause the much-heralded plane's return was off to a poor start.

The F-111 had the potential to be a difference-maker and was part of the push to upgrade the Seventh Air Force's all-weather capability and increase its lagging sortie rate. Using state-of-the-art terrain-following technology the plane was designed to fly at night a mere 200 feet above ground level at nearly the speed of sound and could deliver up to 24 conventional 500-pound bombs or 16 cluster bombs accurately on target. Its ability to strike suddenly without warning and quickly depart allowed it to overcome air defenses at will. Appropriately, the North Vietnamese nicknamed the plane "whispering death." Still, it was dangerous work. As one squadron's bulletin board warned pilots: "Flak effectiveness is 5%—missile effectiveness is 8%—ground effectiveness is 100%—AVOID GROUND."[11] By October two squadrons totaling 48 F-111s were operating out of Takhli with the 474th TFW, striking airfields, SAM sites, communications facilities, and other well-defended military targets and accounting for half the Air Force sorties into the high-threat Route Packs V and VI.[12]

Late September also saw the replacing at Korat of four F-4D squadrons of the 49th TFW that had previously been rushed to Thailand with the new A-7D (the Air Force version of the Navy Corsair II). By mid-October three A-7D squadrons were flying combat mission over North and South Vietnam as part of the 354th TFW. The introduction of the A-7D not only improved the ground attack capability of the Seventh Air Force, but its ability to reach North Vietnamese targets without aerial refueling permitted the reduction of the tanker fleet by nearly 50 planes.[13] Similarly, the Air Force's modification of three

The introduction of the A-7D in September and October 1972 added additional punch to the Air Force's close air support and strike capability in both South Vietnam and the southern panhandle of North Vietnam. (Photo National Museum of the U.S. Air Force)

The USS *Midway* heads toward the Gulf of Tonkin in early 1972 with its complement of A-6, A-7, and F-4 aircraft. The *Midway* and Air Wing 5 would spend over 200 days on the line from April 1972 to February 1973, shooting down four MiG fighters, but also losing 15 aircraft and six pilots in combat. (Photo National Archives)

dozen F-4C Phantoms into Wild Weasel aircraft in 1972 allowed General Vogt to grow the number of hunter-killer teams supporting Linebacker missions. In early October, 18 of these new F-4C Wild Weasels with the 67th TFS arrived at Korat. Although not as sophisticated or well-equipped as the existing F-105Gs, as they were unable to provide distance to a radar site or carry the AGM-78 missile for instance, their addition would ease the work burden and replace losses by nearly doubling the Wild Weasel fleet to a total of 40 aircraft; the F-4Cs would fly 460 sorties over the North from October to January 1973.[14]

Even more critical than the arrival of new reinforcements was the mounting success of the Air Force and Navy in establishing near complete air superiority over the North and eviscerating Hanoi's air defenses in the air and on the ground to the point that no target was safe from the unrelenting wrath of American aerial firepower.

The once dangerous MiG threat in particular had largely been neutralized as the campaign moved toward its climax. American air crews had gained the upper hand in air-to-air combat, because of vastly improved tactics, increased specialization and combat experience, and more effective air warning and control systems. In contrast, the North's inability to replace the loss of experienced pilots and advanced aircraft, chronic maintenance problems, and the ineffectiveness of its older MiG-17 inventory put it on the losing end of the aerial battle of attrition with the Americans. During September and October,

U.S. pilots downed 16 enemy fighters (12 MiG-21s and four MiG-19s) in air-to-air combat; all but one of them being brought down by Phantoms from the Air Force's 432rd TRW and 388th TFW, while losing only two F-4s to their opponents.[15] This put the North's fighter losses at 62 since the beginning of Linebacker; about half its MiG-21s and many of its best pilots were now gone.[16] Perhaps more tellingly, the bulk of VPAF fighter force—its aging MiG-17 units—now seldom challenged the Americans. Their only success came in early July when a plane from the 923rd Fighter Regiment shot down a Navy F-4J off the USS *Saratoga* with cannon fire during a dogfight over Kep.[17] Shortly thereafter, Hanoi tacitly acknowledged that the planes were a non-factor and began shifting resources from them to support MiG-21 and MiG-19 operations.

Likewise, Hanoi's much vaunted surface-to-air defenses began to show signs of strain as the campaign dragged on. Dozens of surface-to-air missile batteries and anti-aircraft emplacements, along with radar tracking and communication sites from the panhandle to Hanoi and Haiphong had been either destroyed or heavily damaged under the weight of nearly six months of bombing. Air Force Wild Weasel hunter-killer teams and Navy Iron Hands not only flew strike support missions, but they also independently

Targeting the North Vietnamese electrical grid, thermal power plants like this one at Nam Dinh southwest of Haiphong came under increasing attack as the intensity of the air campaign increased. (Photo Naval History and Heritage Command)

Old school, the USS *Hancock* on station during Linebacker I and flying the A-4 Skyhawk and the F-8 Crusader much as it did during the ship's very first Vietnam deployment in November 1964. (Photo National Archives)

sought out and attacked SAM sites and threatening anti-aircraft positions wherever they found them. It was, however, the naval blockade and the interdiction effort against overland supply routes from China that had the most crippling impact. With the closure of its ports, Hanoi had to rely on Soviet military resupply through China, which was increasingly problematic given growing strains in the Sino-Soviet relationship and the American focus on interdicting Chinese–North Vietnamese rail and road traffic. By October, it appeared that the North Vietnamese had expended nearly their entire inventory of SA-2 missiles and shortages of anti-aircraft ammunition, especially for larger-caliber weapons over 85-mm, were growing more acute.[18]

This became readily apparent in the steady decline of SA-2 firings as Hanoi was forced to conserve its diminishing missile inventories. Unguided barrage firings became less common and North Vietnamese defenders also appeared to be more selective in when they opted to engage attacking forces. Not surprisingly, U.S. aircraft losses to SAMs showed a consistent downward trend; half as many American planes were lost in September and October than in the first two months of Linebacker.[19] Although improved ECM equipment and anti-SAM tactics likely also contributed to the reduced losses, the decreasing number of missile launches was undeniably a significant factor.

American air commanders, however, were not about to let up and had the full support of the White House to prosecute the war with unrelenting vigor. Early October saw some of the heaviest attacks on North Vietnamese airfields during the campaign in which Phuc

While the more advanced A-6s and A-7s carried the burden of the bombing north of the 20th parallel, the venerable A-4 Skyhawk continued to do yeoman service attacking less well-defended targets in the southern panhandle right up until the ceasefire. (Photo U.S. Navy)

Yen, Yen Bai, Vinh, and Quang Lang were all struck on a single day; five MiGs were caught on the ground and destroyed and another nine were reportedly damaged.[20] On October 6, Admiral Noel Gayler took over from Admiral McCain as Commander-in-Chief, Pacific Fleet and ordered a prioritization of air operations against the North's transportation system and electrical power grid. To support this reenergized effort, Gayler modified the route pack structure by creating an "integrated strike zone" from Route Packs VI a and VI b that included both the northeast and northwest rail lines and the area around Hanoi so as to bring the necessary force to bear to ensure success.[21]

October Breakthrough

Even the air war raging, there was growing optimism in Washington and Hanoi that a peace settlement was finally now within reach as both sides realized that diplomacy was "the best means for ending the war on the most favorable terms they could hope to achieve."[22] For Le Duan and the politburo, the confluence of the failure of the Easter Offensive and the upcoming U.S. presidential election in November gave it a new sense of urgency. Failure to reach some kind of settlement before Nixon's reelection—which the North Vietnamese saw as all but certain by this time—might risk an even more extreme

U.S. military response. Washington, for its part, had some leverage at the moment thanks to the vastly improved military situation in the South and the success of the Linebacker bombing campaign. But time was of the essence for the White House. The ongoing unilateral U.S troop withdrawal and the constant threat of a congressional cutoff of war funding meant this leverage could quickly evaporate. Both sides had much to lose, yet everything to gain from reaching an agreement now.

Thus properly incentive by their respective governments, Kissinger, Xuan Thuy, and Le Duc Tho worked throughout late September and early October to find creative ways to overcome, or at least paper over, their differences in the search for a peace settlement. Increasingly the concerns of both the Saigon government and the Viet Cong were being swept aside in the name of expediency. On October 8 the North Vietnamese delegation handed Kissinger and his deputy Alexander Haig a draft agreement of the minimum terms that Hanoi would accept, one "aimed at ending the American military involvement and providing for a number of principles regarding the internal problems of South Vietnam."[23] It was a turning point in the Paris talks. The North was now willing to make significant political concessions to Washington in the belief that ultimately it would triumph once the Americans were completely out of Vietnam. Importantly, there was Hanoi's tacit acceptance of Kissinger's two-track approach that did not make a ceasefire contingent on a political solution, but Tho did insist that the accord be signed by October 31.

The proposal, entitled "Agreement on Ending the War and Restoring Peace in Vietnam," called for an immediate ceasefire in place without waiting for all political issues to be resolved first; a total withdrawal of all American forces from South Vietnam, while implicitly allowing North Vietnamese troop to remain there; the return of all American POWs within 60 days; an implied, but murky commitment by Hanoi not to infiltrate more troop into the South; and the right of the United States to continue to aid the South Vietnamese and for North Vietnam to do the same for the Viet Cong. In addition, it call for the creation of an "Administration of National Concord" that would organize elections and make decisions by consensus, but not displace the authority of the Saigon government or Provisional Revolutionary Council (the Viet Cong), each of whom would run things in areas it currently controlled.[24] Most significantly, the North had abandoned its demand that President Thieu be removed and a coalition government installed in the South. It also omitted several other divisive and sensitive issues that could be addressed later, such as the presence of North Vietnamese troops in Cambodia and Laos.[25] As lead negotiator Kissinger was more than pleased at the North's change of heart and anticipated a major breakthrough.

The Paris talks now kicked into high gear. Over the course of the next four days beginning on October 8 and ending with a marathon 16-hour session on October 11, a tentative peace agreement was hammered out between Kissinger and Tho. The final product consisted of a 58-page draft that had nine chapters and 18 associated articles for all four parties—the United States, North Vietnam, South Vietnam, and the Provisional Revolutionary Council—to sign. Despite the achievement, it was somewhat anticlimactic for Kissinger. "For nearly four years we longed for this day, yet when it arrived, it was less dramatic than we had ever imagined. Peace came in the guise of the droning voice of an elderly revolutionary wrapping the end of a decade of bloodshed into legalistic ambiguity," he later wrote.[26] Still there were some concerns among the U.S. delegation that while the draft agreement met American requirements for peace with honor it would be a tough sell in Saigon. This would prove to be prophetic.

In the final stages of the negotiations Kissinger requested that Nixon restrict the bombing campaign as a sign of American good will. Nixon agreed and ordered Admiral Gayler on October 14 to cut the sortie rate to 200 in Route Packs V and VI (although the actual number being flown was less than that amount) and a further reduction to 150 was made two days later, which was just above the actual rate at the time.[27] With the finishing touches on the agreement coming together, the White House ordered a complete halt to all Operation Linebacker bombing north of the 20th parallel on October 23. Significantly, air operations south of the 20th parallel would continue, albeit at a reduced level.

During the course of the five-and-a-half-month campaign American pilots flew nearly 42,000 sorties against the North, dropping 155,548 tons of bombs; B-52 bombing of the southern panhandle contributed greatly to this tonnage figure.[28] Overall the Navy flew 57 percent of the sorties, including close to 7,900 at night. The lower Air Force sortie percentage reflected in part its emphasis on conducting highly directed laser-guided bombing missions rather than multiple conventional bombing sorties throughout the campaign. The Americans lost at total of 89 aircraft, split 45 to 44 between the Navy and Air Force. The majority of Air Force losses were to MiG fighters—61 percent—while the majority of Navy losses were to defensive fire—60 percent—reflecting each service's contrasting role and operational area focus.[29] Despite some teething problems, Linebacker was deemed a success. It had helped stem the flow of men and matériel southward to the battlefield. It vastly restricted overseas resupply coming into the country and heavily damaged the North's military and economic infrastructure. Most important, it was seen as a key factor in driving Hanoi toward a peace settlement. But would it be enough to finally end the war?

Oh So Close

The mood in Washington and Hanoi was celebratory as the momentum for finalizing a settlement seemed unstoppable, so much so that Kissinger publicly declared in Paris on October 26 that "peace is at hand." Kissinger's keen optimism was somewhat surprising given his visit to Saigon the previous week to discuss the terms of the proposed agreement. It did not go well.

The White House's desire to keep the Paris negotiations out of the limelight and Kissinger's secretive and close-to-the-vest negotiating style already had left many in Saigon feeling isolated and neglected. These insecurities were further compounded when President Thieu first learned about terms of the draft peace agreement, not from the Americans, but from documents captured by South Vietnamese intelligence in the days leading up to Kissinger's October 19 visit.[30] Thieu and his closest advisers were incensed. They saw the agreement as an utter betrayal that gave far too many concessions to Hanoi by permitting North Vietnamese troops to remain in the South, by failing to create a secure DMZ that would prevent resupply and troop movements, and in allowing the inclusion of a national council of reconciliation that smacked of a coalition government. It was seen as "tantamount to surrender" and a death sentence on the Saigon government.[31]

Over the course of the next several days, Kissinger, senior American diplomats, and U.S. military officers sought to assuage Thieu's anger and overcome South Vietnamese feelings of distrust and abandonment through a carrot-and-stick approach.

The Nixon administration, which had already committed itself to replacing South Vietnamese equipment and material losses from the Easter Offensive, used the entice-ment of vastly accelerated military deliveries to gain Thieu's acquiescence. Under the name of Project Enhance Plus (Project Enhance was the existing program for replacing military equipment losses on a one-to-one basis), Washington sought to boost Saigon's military capabilities and provide it with a stockpile of equipment to defend itself after the American withdrawal. This golden handshake was to consist of nearly 300 fighter-bomb-ers (including more than 100 advanced F-5s), the transfer of all existing A-1 aircraft in Southeast Asia to the VNAF, 227 UH-1 helicopters, 32 C-130s, 200 armored vehicles, equip-ment for three artillery battalions, and 2,000 trucks, as well as large quantities of spare parts, ammunition, and POL products.[32] Enhanced Plus was not without its critics, with American military officers pointing out that it would years for the South Vietnamese mil-itary to absorb this much equipment. In particular, the goal of creating a 20-squadron ground attack air force might take over five years and would likely lead to a degradation in VNAF capabilities in the near term.[33]

Kissinger also worked to coax the South Vietnamese toward acceptance. He pledged wording changes to address their concerns and told Thieu that he had no reason to fear North Vietnamese forces remaining in the South, because Washington would "enforce the settlement" in the case of any massive violation.[34] Likewise, General Abrams, as MACV commander, added his personal assurance by saying that President Nixon's commitment to South Vietnam was firm and that the military situation in the South was now secure.[35] Kissinger, however, was not beyond applying strong-arm tactics as well. On October 21 he handed Thieu a letter from Nixon saying that "were you to find the agreement to be unacceptable at this point" in light of concessions by the North, "it is my judgement that your decision would have the most serious effects upon my ability to continue to provide support for you and for the Government of South Vietnam."[36] American military aid was on the line and Saigon was embarking on a suicidal course warned Kissinger. But still Thieu resisted.

Meanwhile, frustration at the delay was boiling over in Hanoi. Le Duan and the polit-buro were growing increasingly annoyed with the Americans over the objections now being raised by Saigon when they believed that the agreement was complete. Moreover, Moscow and Beijing were insisting that Hanoi sign and not jeopardize this opportunity to end the war.[37] Seeking to shift the pressure back to Washington and Saigon, the North Vietnamese on October 25 released a chronology of the Paris talks, the key terms of the agreement, and the now abandoned timetable for signing. Kissinger tried to put the best face on things and paint an optimistic picture, but he knew better. Amid Thieu's intransi-gence and Hanoi's rehardening of its position, the best chance for peace in four years had just slipped through the American's hands. It was now back to the drawing board.

6. UNLEASHING THE DOGS OF WAR

The disappointment in failing to finalize a settlement cast a dark pall over peace talks and set the stage for a return to protracted negotiations as each blamed the other for the October débâcle. Moreover, the talks regressed as positions hardened. Previous concessions made by both sides were withdrawn and any good will between Kissinger and Tho seemingly evaporated. Apparently it was back to square one.

After some delay the talks resumed in Paris on November 20 in an effort to salvage the key elements of the draft agreement. Kissinger's presentation of Thieu's lengthy list of 69 demands, however, was met with cold disdain by Tho, who countered by presenting his own set of demands that now included tying the release of American prisoners of war to concessions from Saigon.[1] Hanoi also refused to discuss the withdrawal of North Vietnamese troops from the South, which was a non-negotiable demand of the Thieu government. Things only got worse, the following sessions "degenerating into stonewalling, pounding fists, and issuing of threats," with the latter including a threat by Nixon to resume military activities if the North refused to negotiate seriously.[2]

Washington's patience with Saigon was also wearing thin. Kissinger was increasingly fearful that "Thieu's intransigence in October may well have lost us a unique opportunity to arrive at a settlement."[3] Building U.S. congressional opposition to funding the war limited his room for maneuver and the South Vietnamese delegation in Paris constantly hovered over Kissinger's shoulder, fearful that he would once again betray them. Complicating things further, the Thieu government launched an obstructionist public relations campaign in mid-December to derail the peace process and further undermine any chance of a settlement. With the talks stalled, Tho left for Hanoi on December 14 to consult with the North Vietnamese leadership.

Nixon and Kissinger were at the end of their rope. The American involvement in Vietnam was coming to an end and Washington needed to reach a peace agreement—one way or another. To incentivize Hanoi, while also reassuring Saigon, the White House moved once again toward using military muscle to break the deadlock. The deadline for finalizing a reasonable agreement was fast approaching. Hanoi and Saigon could be a helpful part of the process or face the consequences of an American-imposed version: the choice was theirs. On December 14 Nixon sent Hanoi an ultimatum to return to the talks within 72 hours or suffer the consequences. The day of reckoning was fast approaching.

Preparing for Renewed Hostilities

While Kissinger was searching desperately for a diplomatic solution, American military commanders were making plans for a renewed bombing north of the 20th parallel at the direction of the President. As negotiations broke down in December Alexander Haig was able to convince Nixon that only massive bombing would bring Hanoi around; the United States must "strike hard at its heart and keep on striking until the enemy's will was broken."[4] Feeling backed into a corner with little choice at this point, Nixon decided to go ahead and prepare to unleash the most powerful air campaign of the war.

The White House's weapon of choice would be the B-52 Stratofortress, which for the first time since the one-off Freedom Porch Bravo raid against Haiphong in April 1972 would be used against the North's heartland. Its all-weather capability and tremendous payload made it the ideal airframe for the envisioned bombing campaign. But it was the overwhelming psychological impact of wave after wave of the big bombers dropping their deadly loads on Hanoi and Haiphong that was most appealing to Nixon. It sent an unmistakable message of American resolve to end the war. It was also not, however, without considerable risk. While B-52s had been extensively used since 1965 in a tactical support role in the form of Arc Light missions and had played a critical role in halting the Easter Offensive in the South, they had been used only sparingly over North Vietnam itself, confined to the lower air-threat environment of the southern panhandle. Nonetheless, as the Linebacker campaign gained steam in the late summer and fall, the selective use of B-52s had expanded to include bombing missions up to the 20th parallel by early November.[5] Now, however, the bombers would be tasked with flying directly into the teeth of the North's air defenses.

The Air Force had been planning this for some time. Beginning in the spring of 1972 the Air Force began augmenting its modest B-52 force and KC-135 tanker fleet presence in Southeast Asia under Operation Bullet Shot. The process accelerated dramatically in April as General Abrams requested additional Arc Light support to counter the Easter Offensive. Soon the airfields at U-Tapao, Thailand, and Guam's Andersen Air Force Base would be at maximum B-52 capacity with a combined total of 140 bombers.[6] And still even more aircraft would be flown into the theater at the behest of the White House given Nixon's fixation with increasing the size of the bomber force in Southeast Asia.

By mid-December 1972, the Strategic Air Command had mustered a total of 206 B-52s at its bases on Guam and in Thailand. (Photo National Museum of the U.S. Air Force)

Guam: America's Rock of the Pacific

Since its acquisition from Spain following the Spanish-American War in 1898 the island of Guam steadily emerged as a vital base for U.S. military power projection in the western Pacific and Southeast Asia. With the rising American involvement in Vietnam in the 1960s the island became an important logistics base and home to a growing Air Force presence with the expansion of Andersen Air Force Base's bomber and tanker fleet. By mid-1965, B-52F bombers out of Guam were regularly flying the 5,200-mile, 12–14-hour round trip to South Vietnam on Arc Light bombing missions. Nothing however could have prepared the island for the prominent role it would assume in the final year of America's Vietnam involvement.

In January 1972, amid concern by military commanders of growing enemy activity in the face of American ground troop withdrawals from South Vietnam, the Joint Chiefs authorized the augmentation of the B-52 presence in Southeast Asia, which had dwindled to about 40 planes. As part of Operation Bullet Shot the Strategic Air Command (SAC) undertook the transfer of B-52s from mainland United States to Thailand and Guam. The task gained greater urgency with the outbreak of the Easter Offensive on March 30 and the need for greatly increased B-52 sortie rates. Over the course of several phases SAC rebuilt its bomber forces to 58 B-52Ds and 28 B-52Gs at Andersen and 54 B-52Ds at U-Tapao, Thailand, by the summer. At the behest of higher command authority, SAC authorized the transfer of an additional 72 B-52Gs to Guam to push the number of bombers in theater to more than two hundred.

This rapid influx of aircraft and personnel soon had "The Rock" (Guam's nickname) bursting at the seams. One of the Andersen's runways was closed to park the additional aircraft and a maintenance wing was stood up in July. More than 12,000 arriving airmen overpowered the base's infrastructure forcing thousands to be housed in converted buildings, "tin cities" or even tent shelters, creating the largest Air Force presence on the island since the end of World War II.

In addition to flying Arc Light missions against attacking North Vietnamese forces as part of the American air response to Hanoi's offensive in the South, B-52s in April began bombing barracks, ammunition and supply depots, POL storage facilities, and key road junctions across the southern panhandle of North Vietnam as part of the U.S. interdiction effort. These were the first B-52 strikes on North Vietnam since October 1968. The sorties rate out of Guam continued to rise as Operation Linebacker I gained momentum in May, but concerns over the vulnerability of the big bombers to North Vietnamese air defenses limited their use to south of the 20th parallel. All this changed, however, in mid-December when President Nixon ordered an intensified bombing offensive against Hanoi and Haiphong using B-52s for the first time. Operation Linebacker II got underway on December 18 and would last until December 29. During the course of the campaign B-52 crews out of Guam would fly 54 percent of the 729 B-52 combat sorties and helped to deliver the 15,237 tons of munitions dropped by B-52s. It would cost the men of "The Rock" seven planes and 17 airmen killed along with another 14 captured.

Even after the signing of the Paris peace accords on January 23, 1973, bombers out of Andersen continued to fly missions against targets in Cambodia and Laos until August 1973 with no aircraft losses. With the winding down of American engagement in Southeast Asia, all B-52 operations on Guam came to an end; all remaining bombers on the island were redeployed by the end of 1973.

The 57th Air Division (Provisional) on Guam only did manage to absorb another 58 B-52s (of the additional 100 Nixon wanted) by closing down one of Andersen's two runways and then using it to park the additional aircraft.[7] At the time the decision was made to begin a new bombing campaign in December 1972, the Air Force could muster 206 B-52 bombers in theater—54 B-52Ds at U-Tapao, 99 B-52Gs and 53 B-52Ds at Andersen[8]—which was nearly half the Strategic Air Command's (SAC) entire bomber inventory at the time.[9]

Planning responsibility for the new air campaign, codename Linebacker II,[10] was given to the Commander-in-Chief of Strategic Air Command, General John Meyer, and his headquarters staff at Offutt Air Force Base, just outside of Omaha, Nebraska—some 8,000 miles from the war zone—and bypassed air commanders in the field. Preparation for a maximum bombing effort had actually been underway at Offutt since late summer and so the SAC staff was ready with a list of about 60 targets suitable for bombing by B-52s in Route Pack VI.[11] The list included airfields, railyards, POL storage facilities, power plants, large

The Air Force relied on hundreds of KC-135 tankers based in Southeast Asia to provide the aerial refueling capability necessary to support Linebacker II operations.

military warehouses, and transshipment points; all were readily identifiable to radar or were sufficiently large to be attacked by a three-ship B-52 cell with little likelihood that the bombs would fall outside the target box.[12] Things were put on hold following the bombing halt north of the 20th parallel in late October as it appeared a breakthrough in Paris was imminent, but now it was time to dust off the list.

While SAC's B-52 force would be the centerpiece of the Linebacker II bombing effort, Air Force and Navy tactical strike aircraft, such as the F-111, A-6, and A-7, were also slated to play a major role in the campaign. The B-52s would attack at night and then tactical strikes by the Seventh Air Force and Task Force 77 would follow up during the day to maintain round-the-clock pressure on Hanoi and Haiphong. In addition to the strike aircraft, greater numbers than ever before of supporting planes would be required to accompany the B-52 strike packages. In all the American air order of battle would top 1,300 planes.[13]

The North Vietnamese were also busily preparing for another round of American bombing. They took advantage of the nearly two-month bombing hiatus to repair damaged infrastructure, rebuild and resupply their air defenses, and plan for the expected American air assault. Even more so than during Linebacker I, surface-to-air missiles became the lynchpin of the North's defenses; an estimated 200 SA-2 launchers were concentrated around the Hanoi-Haiphong heartland. Thanks to an aggressive resupply effort, Hanoi was thought to have stockpiled some 2,300 SA-2 missiles in its arsenal by mid-December.[14] Still North

General John Meyer, the head of the Strategic Air Command, was responsible for drawing up the initial battle plan for the White House's December bombing campaign that was designed to send an unmistakable ultimatum to Hanoi. (Photo U.S. Air Force)

Vietnamese defenses were suspect. The once formidable MiG fighter threat had been greatly diminished with only about 80 MiG-21s and MiG-19s believed to be operational.[15] MiG-17s as we have seen were a nonfactor since the summer. Though both Hanoi and Haiphong were encircled by hundreds of anti-aircraft weapons, including radar-controlled 85-mm and 100-mm guns, they did not pose a serious threat to the high-flying B-52s. Ground fire, however, would be a constant worry for Navy and Air Force aircraft flying low-level attack profiles, accounting for the loss of three A-6s and one F-111 during the course of the campaign.[16]

Finally the waiting was over. On December 15 the Joint Chiefs sent notification to Admiral Gayler and General Meyer that they should be ready "for a maximum-effort strike" against targets in North Vietnam.[17] The word was quickly passed down to field

The B-52s of Linebacker II

By 1972 the United States had built up an inventory of approximately 450 B-52 bombers as the central air component of its nuclear triad. Designed originally as an intercontinental, high-altitude nuclear bomber to penetrate Soviet airspace, the eight-engine and nearly 200-ton Stratofortress (nicknamed "Buff" for Big Ugly Fat Fellow) would see extensive use as a conventional bomber in Vietnam. To meet a growing bombing demand, the older B-52D models were modified and upgraded under the Big Belly program in 1966 to increase their conventional internal and external bomb payload to almost 30 tons, improve their electronic systems, and install additional ECM equipment. For most of war their targets were in South Vietnam flying Arc Light missions by which two three-plane cells would saturate an area 1.5 miles long by half a mile wide with bombs, but the Ds would also play a prominent role in Linebacker II.

Supplementing B-52D operations during the war were the longer-range, but smaller-payload (only about one-third the size) B-52Gs that were based out of Andersen Air Force Base on Guam. While faster and able to operate at greater distances, they often lacked the most up-to-date ECM equipment when large numbers of Gs were rushed to Guam from the United States during bomber force buildup following the outbreak of the 1972 Easter Offensive. Both models, however, sported the same six-man crew composition that included an electronic warfare officer responsible for detecting and jamming enemy radars and a tail gunner, who operated either radar-guided quad .50-caliber machine guns (D model) or a 20-mm cannon (G model). The G models would comprise roughly half the B-52 attack force during Linebacker II.

At the start of the air campaign, the 307th Strategic Wing and the 310th Strategic Wing with a total of 54 B-52Ds were based at U-Tapao, Thailand, as part of the 17th Air Division (Provisional) under command of Brigadier General Glenn Sullivan. Another 53 B-52Ds with the 43rd Strategic Wing were based at Andersen Air Force Base on Guam as part of the 57th Air Division (Provisional) under Brigadier General Andrew Anderson. Likewise, the 99 B-52Gs of the 72nd Strategic Wing on Guam also fell under Brigadier General Anderson's command. All B-52 operations in Southeast Asia were overseen by Lieutenant General Gerald Johnson from his Eighth Air Force headquarters on Guam.

By the time the eleven-day campaign was over on December 29 the men of the Eighth Air Force would have completed 729 combat sorties against the heart of the North Vietnamese defenses, delivering 15,237 tons of bombs on 34 targets while having up to 1,200 SA-2 missiles fired at them. Their tail gunners would also down two MiG-21s, the first ever kills by B-52s. But it would cost them 15 aircraft—nine B-52Ds and six B52-Gs—along with 33 crewmembers taken prisoner and another 25 killed or missing in action, doing a job they never expected to do, yet they met the challenge.

commanders with the official orders arriving two days later: "You are directed to commence at approximately 1200z, 18 December 1972 a three-day maximum effort, repeat maximum effort of B-52/TAC Airstrikes in the Hanoi/Haiphong areas against the targets contained in [the authorized target list]. Object is maximum destruction of selected military targets in the vicinity of Hanoi/Haiphong. Be prepared to extend operations past three days, if directed."[18]

The orders went on to authorize the use of "all resources which could be spared" and to "exercise precaution to minimize risk of civilian casualties."[19] At the time of making his decision to move forward with Linebacker II, Nixon reportedly told Admiral Moorer that "I don't want any more of this crap about the fact that we couldn't hit this target or that one. This is your chance to use military power to win this war. And if you don't, I'll hold you responsible."[20] The message was clear: it was now time for American airpower to prove its worth in a decisive fashion.

Launch Operation Linebacker II

The early evening of December 18 saw the commencement of Linebacker II, not with B-52 strikes, but with low-level bombing attacks against five major VPAF airbases in Hanoi's Red River Valley by Air Force F-111 fighter-bombers.[21] Catching the North Vietnamese defenders by surprise, 16 F-111s of the 474th TFW from Takhli dropped 48 tons bombs on the airfields at Bac Mai, Hoa Lac, Kep, Phuc Yen, and Yen Bai. Following the F-111 strikes, Air Force F-4s began laying chaff corridors to and from the target areas, Wild

Weasels took up their positions, as did F-4 fighters providing combat air patrol and EB-66 jammers. In all almost 40 aircraft would be supporting the B-52 strike force,[22] while dozens more planes provided stand-off assistance in the form of aerial refueling, communications and warning, electronic countermeasures, and search and rescue.

The first wave consisting of 18 B-52Gs and 9 B-52Ds from Guam and 21 B-52Ds from U-Tapao linked up over northern Laos to form one continuous line of 48 aircraft grouped into cells of three that were then spaced up to ten minutes apart and stretched more than 70 miles across the sky.[23] Within this formation, nicknamed the "elephant walk," the bombers were divided into attack groups of two to six cells—six to 18 planes—and assigned a target. In keeping with SAC call-sign conventions, each three-plane

Lt Gen Gerald Johnson as commander of the Eight Air Force's B-52 fleet in Southeast Asia was responsible for implementing Linebacker II. (Photo U.S. Air Force)

cell was given a color name, e.g., "White," "Charcoal" or "Brown," but by the end of the campaign SAC mission planners would struggle to come up with different color cell names, forcing them to be creative with names, such as "Plaid," "Snow," and "Topaz." Crossing into North Vietnam the bombers flew northeast before turning southeast over the Red River valley to make their final run toward Hanoi. F-105G Wild Weasels preceded the bombers in an effort to suppress the city's SAM defenses both electronically and by launching missiles at active radar signals. At 1945 hours the first wave started its bombing run.

The targets for the first wave consisted of the airfields at Hao Lac, Kep, and Phuc Yen, as well as the Kinh No and the Yen Vien railyard and storage complexes just north of Hanoi. A total of 21 B-52s hit the three airfields, while the other 27 unloaded their payloads on the two rail complexes. SA-2 missiles and anti-aircraft fire soon lit up the skies, despite the best effort of the Wild Weasel teams to suppress the sites. It was "wall-to-wall SAMs," according to one B-52 pilot, but the bomb-laden planes were under orders to "press on" regardless

Right: Air Force ordnance men at U-Tapao, Thailand preparing a B-52D for a mission.

Below: The up to 18-hour round trip to Hanoi required B-52s from Guam to be refueled by KC-135 tankers on both the inbound and outbound legs of the mission. (Photo U.S. Air Force)

The standard battle formation for B-52 bombers was a three-plane cell with each cell given a different color code name, i.e. Brown 01, Brown 02, and Brown 03.

of the defensive fire.[24] One B-52D from U-Tapao, however, was so seriously damaged by shrapnel from an SA-2 near miss that it was forced to abort and soon another nine-plane formation from the 72nd SW out of Andersen found itself under heavy fire as it was attacking the Yen Vien railyard. A volley of 17 missiles was launched against the last cell of the formation as it prepared to drop its bombs. Two of these missiles hit the fuselage of *Charcoal 01* at 34,000 feet, setting it on fire and knocking the B-52G out of control with it "spinning earthward like a huge burning leaf."[25] Only three of the crew managed to escape the burning inferno before it crashed, becoming the first B-52 prisoners of war.

Meanwhile, several MiG-21s were able to get airborne despite the airfield attacks to threaten the bombers, as well as the EB-66 jammers south of Hanoi. This resulted in at least three air-to-air engagements with F-4 fighters, but no kills were recorded by either side. It did, however, add to the confusion in the skies, as fighter escorts struggled to protect the bombers without becoming victims themselves of trigger-happy B-52 tail gunners. There was no such confusion for the turret gunner in *Brown 03*, a B-52D of the 307rd SW out of U-Tapao. Staff Sergeant Samuel Turner was able to shoot down an attacking MiG-21 with his radar-controlled .50-caliber machine guns—the first by a B-52 tail gunner.[26] Turner was later awarded a Silver Star for his accomplishment.

The second wave of 30 B-52s out of Guam rolled in just after midnight to restrike the Kinh No and the Yen Vien complexes, as well as bomb the railyard and repair facility just east of the Red River from downtown Hanoi. Once again the bombers were preceded by F-4s laying chaff corridors, F-105G Wild Weasels striking and jamming SAM sites, and F-4s flying combat air patrol. Still the North Vietnamese defenders were able to launch 68 missiles into the night sky;[27] one explosion critically damaging a B-52G of the 72nd SW following its attack on Kinh No. Its left wing badly damaged and on fire, two engines gone, and streaming fuel, Major Cliff Ashley just barely coaxed the burning plane across the Thai border before the crew was forced to abandon the aircraft. All crew members were successfully rescued.[28]

Just before dawn the third and final wave struck. It was also the largest of the first day's attacks with 51 aircraft—30 from Andersen and 21 from U-Tapao—attacking the Hanoi Radio facility on the outskirts of the city for the first time, as well as again striking the Hanoi and Kinh No railyard complexes. Even though Navy A-7 Iron Hands took over the SAM-suppression duties from the overworked Wild Weasels, the North Vietnamese defenders were able to launch more than 150 missiles against the American attackers.[29] They were

Above left: Overconfidence and predictable routes and timing in the initial days of Linebacker II produced disturbing B-52 losses: nine bombers in the first three days.

Above right: Civilians and militia examine wreckage from a B-52 shot down during an attack on the Bac Mai airfield complex near Hanoi on the night of December 21, 1972.

successful in shooting down one B-52D attached to the 307th SW out of U-Tapao; two crewmen died and four were captured after ejecting.[30] Another B-52D from the 43rd SW out of Guam was damaged by a near miss from an SA-2 while attacking the Radio Hanoi site, but was able to divert and land safely back in Thailand. A few MiGs briefly attempted to engage the strike force, but escorting Phantoms quickly drove them off.

As daylight broke over Hanoi, clouds of smoke continued to bellow from the aftermath of the night's raids and the full implication of the bombing began to register on the North Vietnamese leadership and the city's residents. This American air campaign was clearly different. Nixon had now shown he was willing to risk sending his largest and most lethal bomber force against the North's heartland, flying 121 B-52 sorties that first night. The North in return had fired off more than 200 SA-2 missiles, downing three bombers and damaging two others.[31] And the battle was just the beginning.

December 19 saw the opening round of daytime tactical airstrikes by Air Force and Navy aircraft that would establish an alternating pattern during the campaign. Large nighttime B-52 raids, accompanied by selective F-111 and A-6 attacks against airfields, military communication centers, and air defenses, that would then be followed by a series of daytime tactical strikes to produce a near constant level of bombardment against the Hanoi-Haiphong area. The goal, as much political and psychological as military, was to inflict as much damage as possible on the North's war-making capability, while also stoking fear in the North Vietnamese populace and pressuring Hanoi into resuming

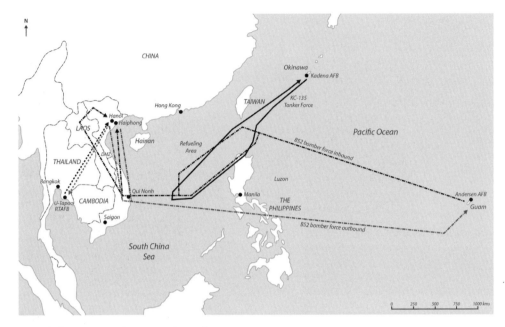

B-52 Flight Routes and Support Aircraft Locations.

negotiations. Unfortunately, the notoriously poor December weather conditions over the target region often prevented the Air Force from using laser-guided munitions, forced multiple mission cancellations, and shifted the burden to LORAN-equipped F-4 aircraft as strike leads for radar bombing with conventional bombs.[32] All tactical strike packages were likewise supported by chaff bombers, fighter escorts, Wild Weasels, and ECM aircraft mimicking the successful Linebacker I tactics, even though this put severe strain on resources that were also needed to support the nightly B-52 sorties. Over the course of the next several days, A-7Ds with the 354th out of Korat and F-4s out of Ubon attached to the 8th TFW struck airfields, railyards, radio and communication sites, and power plants. The airfield at Yen Bai, which sat astride the primary B-52 ingress route about 70 miles northwest of Hanoi, was hit twice by a total of 40 Air Force A-7s on December 19 and 20. Also on the 20th, 54 F-4s using radar bombing struck Hanoi main radio and communication facilities, causing significant damage. On December 21, 46 F-4s and 16 A-7s bombed multiple railyards east and south of the city, inflicting heavy damage. Improving weather also allowed 8th TFW pilots to destroy Hanoi's main rail station and completely knock out its downtown thermal power plant with eight laser-guided MK-84 2,000-pound bombs.[33] The attackers suffered no losses, encountering only anti-aircraft defensive fire; SA-2 missiles were apparently being saved for use against the B-52s.

Meanwhile, A-6 and A-7 aircraft from the *America, Enterprise, Midway,* and *Ranger* were busy attacking a variety of targets in the Haiphong area, as well along the coastline from Cam Pha to Thanh Hoa both day and night. North Vietnamese air defenses were often priority targets. The airfields at Kep and Kien An were repeatedly struck as were SAM sites.

Above: As a MiG-21 pilot with the 921st Fighter Regiment, Do Van Lanh, would score four air combat victories, but he and other MiG-21 pilots failed to down any B-52s during Linebacker II. (Photo National Museum of the U.S. Air Force)

Right: Master Sergeant Louis LeBlanc is taken prisoner following the downing of his U-Tapao-based B-52D by a surface-to-air missile on the night of December 22 northwest of Hanoi. During Operation Homecoming in February and March 1973, 33 B-52 crew members would be among those POWs released.

In one large raid, ten sites in the Haiphong area were hit by Intruders from the *America* and *Ranger* on the night of December 20.[34] Despite the strong defenses, Navy losses were light. One A-7C Iron Hand was lost to an SA-2 missile while contesting a SAM site south of Haiphong on December 19 and an A-6A Intruder off the *Enterprise* was lost the next night to 37-mm anti-aircraft fire while making a low-level bombing run against the Haiphong shipyards.[35] Both pilots and the Intruder's bombardier/navigator were taken prisoner.

In addition to their bombing and SAM-suppression missions, Navy aircraft were ordered to reseed the minefields around the Haiphong and Hon Gai harbors, as well as those blocking smaller ports and river estuaries as far south as Dong Hoi, to ensure the effectiveness of the naval blockade. The first Operation Pocket Money fields were laid in early May with the commencement of Linebacker I, but had been set to deactivate after six months and, moreover, a series of extremely strong solar flares in August caused the premature detonation of over 4,000 of the roughly 8,000 MK-36 DST magnetic mines.[36] Accordingly, on December 19, A-7Es from CVW-2 off the *Ranger*, carrying ten mines each began the process of reseeding the fields in Haiphong and Hon Gai harbors and their channel approaches, a process that would continue over the next several days. No planes were lost until December 24 when an A-7E from VA-113 was shot down by apparent anti-aircraft fire and the pilot killed.[37] By the end of December, all the minefields from Cam Pha to Dong Hoi had been successfully reseeded without any further loss of aircraft.

Above: The radar-controlled quad .50-caliber tail guns of the B-52D proved successful in not only thwarting MiG attacks, but in shooting down two of the fighters during Linebacker II. (Photo National Museum of the U.S. Air Force)

Below: General John Meyer presents Staff Sergeant Samuel Turner with a Silver Star for his shooting down of a MiG-21 on the night December 18, 1972. This was the first downing of an enemy aircraft by a B-52 tail gunner. (Photo National Museum of the U.S. Air Force)

The real focus of the campaign, however, was on the B-52 strikes and the compelling message Washington was intending to send to Hanoi. On December 19 the ongoing operation was extended indefinitely by President Nixon. The days leading up to Christmas would see dramatic swings in the air campaign and raise serious questions about U.S. tactics, as well as American resolve. Ultimately, this period would prove to be a turning point for Linebacker II.

Toward A Turning Point

Building on the initial success of the first missions and what General Meyer considered acceptable losses, Eighth Air Force commander, Lieutenant General Gerald Johnson, pressed forward with repeat performances on the nights of December 19 and 20. Ninety-three bombers in three waves—27 B-52Ds and 36 B-52Gs from Andersen and 30 B-52Ds from U-Tapao—once again struck targets in the Hanoi area on the 19th, including Yen Vien and Kinh No railyard complexes and the Hanoi Radio facility for the second night, as well as the Thai Nguyen thermal power plant and Bac Giang transshipment point located farther north and northeast of the city.[38] The support aircraft composition, routing, and even timing of the waves mirrored the previous night. No MiG fighters rose to attack the bombers, thanks in part to preemptive F-111 "whispering death" strikes against Hanoi's airfields, but the SAM batteries were as active as ever despite the best efforts of the F-105G and F-4C Wild Weasels and Navy A-6 Iron

Hands. More than 180 SA-2 were fired. Two B-52s were damaged, one so seriously that it barely made it back to Thai airspace before making an emergency landing at Nam Phong.[39]

Just as the last planes of the third wave were landing on Guam on the 20th following their grueling 18-hour roundtrip, the evening's strike force was warming up its engines in preparation for takeoff. With no real time to adjust mission procedures and a degree of overconfidence, the third day's tactics and maneuvers remained basically the same that could best be described as a composite of routes, targets, and tactics from the previous days.[40] But the North Vietnamese defenders were learning fast and the bomber crews flying on the night of December 20 were in for a rude awakening.

Right: B-52s queue up on the runway at Andersen AFB, Guam, prior to a Linebacker II mission. (Photo U.S. Air Force)

Below: B-52Gs taking off from Andersen Air Force Base, December 1972. Although they comprised nearly half the bomber fleet, many of the G models lacked the modified electronic countermeasures equipment needed to protect them against SA-2 missiles. (Photo U.S. Air Force)

The targets that night would be familiar ones for the 99-plane strike force from Andersen and U-Tapao. As on previous nights, F-111 strikes against airfields and military communications sites and F-4s dropping chaff opened the way for the bombers, while Wild Weasels, F-4 fighters, and EB-66 jammers took up their supporting positions. The first wave consisting of 33 aircraft—six B52-Ds and 12 B-52-Gs from Andersen, along with 15 B-52Ds from U-Tapao—made the now well-worn approach along the Red River into the Hanoi area in the early evening hours.[41] First up was the Hanoi railyard and repair facility. Surprisingly, the six bombers encountered few missile firings despite the high level of enemy electronic activity. It was, however, to be a vastly different story for the remaining 27 planes that pressed on to attack the Yen Vien rail complex and an adjacent warehouse facility. Lying in wait, the North Vietnamese SA-2 batteries suddenly unleashed at least 130 missiles against the B-52s over the course of their bombing runs.[42] In short order, three bombers were fatally hit by exploding missiles (one had already been damaged by MiG-21 cannon fire). Two went down immediately over Hanoi, while the other reached Thailand before crashing.[43]

Shocked by the losses in the first wave and especially with concerns for B-52Gs with their inferior ECM equipment, the attack by six B-52Gs from the second wave on Hanoi's railyard was aborted. The other 21 bombers struck the Thai Nguyen thermal power plant 40 miles north of the city and Bac Giang railyard 30 miles to the northeast. Before daybreak, on schedule, and with the North Vietnamese gunners waiting, the third wave of 39 bombers struck Hanoi's Gia Lam railyard and repair facility, a Hanoi POL storage site, and the Kinh No railyard complex, as well as the Bac Giang transshipment point.[44] During the attack on Kinh No two B-52Gs were hit by SA-2s, both catching fire and crashing in flames. Only four of the 13 crewmen on board the planes survived to be taken prisoner. A B-52D from the 43rd SW out of Guam was also hit and badly damaged shortly after dropping its payload on the Gia Lam railyard, but still managed to cross into Laos before it became uncontrollable and was abandoned. Five of the six crewmen were rescued with the sixth listed as missing presumed dead.[45]

F-111As armed with 500-pound bombs were used extensively to strike North Vietnamese airfields, air defense sites, and communication facilities in advance of nighttime B-52 bombing missions during Linebacker II. (Photo National Museum of the U.S. Air Force)

Air Force EB-66 aircraft played an essential role in jamming North Vietnamese air defense systems during the December bombing. (Photo National Museum of the Air Force)

When it was all over the Eighth Air Force had lost six bombers—four B-52Gs and two B-52Ds—and had two more seriously damaged, to make it the darkest day ever for the Strategic Air Command. It was estimated that more than 200 SA-2s had been launched in well-timed and coordinating fashion with MiG-21s, who apparently had been used to shadow the bombers and confirm their altitude, heading, and airspeed to enable blind firing.[46] In the first three nights' bombing, nine B-52s had been lost and several more heavily damaged. Most worrisome was the vulnerability of B-52Gs with inferior ECM equipment and post-bomb-release turn procedures that exposed the bombers to missile attacks.[47] The heavy losses provoked criticism of SAC, with Nixon "raising holy hell" and ordering the Pentagon to correct the situation at once.[48] Air commanders and aircrews also began to openly question the predictable and repetitive strike plans. "The crews were concerned over tactics that we believed injurious to our health," recalled one officer, "and we were very vocal about these in our debriefings."[49]

Fortunately, B-52Ds from the 307th and the 310th strategic wings out of U-Tapao were slated to carry the burden of bombing over the next few days, which gave some breathing room to the 57th Air Division's two wings on Guam.[50] In the meantime, SAC planners worked to address the challenge of better utilizing and protecting the B-52Gs with unmodified ECM equipment that comprised a significant portion of the bomber force, as well as how best to revise battle plans and operational procedures to ensure the success of the campaign. In addition to the obvious issues of predictable routing and timing of the B-52 raids, the first days of campaign brought to light a number of other serious problems with fighter escort and support coordination, ineffective chaff distribution, tactical communications overload, and lack of bomber cell cohesion for mutual ECM support. Most significantly, it was discovered that some North Vietnamese SA-2 batteries were using a modified Fire Can anti-aircraft gun control radar in conjunction with the Fan Song guidance radar to launch very accurate single and paired missiles. The new technique used a passive, guided home-on-jam procedure on an odd frequency that none of the American ECM equipment was designed to counter.[51] Since the White House demanded no letup in the air campaign, something had to be done and fast to rectify these problems.

In the meantime, the B-52D crews out of Thailand along with Air Force and Navy tactical aircraft were expected to carry on as best they could to maintain the momentum. The nighttime B-52 strikes from December 21 to 24 were smaller in size—only 30 planes operating in a single wave—than in the opening days of the campaign and were sent against a diverse set of targets spread widely across Route Pack VI. This change also allowed the Seventh Air Force to up the number of its support aircraft by nearly 20, including additional chaff bombers to increase the area coverage and the addition of night hunter-killer teams by adding F-4Es with cluster bombs to the Wild Weasel flights.[52]

The targets on the 21st were the Quang Te airfield located about 30 miles southwest of Hanoi that was hit by six B-52Ds, along with the Van Dien storage area and Bac Mai airfield and storage complex on the city's southern outskirts, which were both attacked by 12 bombers each. As usual the raid was preceded by low-level F-111 strikes on Hanoi's surrounding airfields, as well as other F-111 sorties against rail facilities and transshipment points north of the city. VPAF fighters made a sporadic appearance, but were run off by

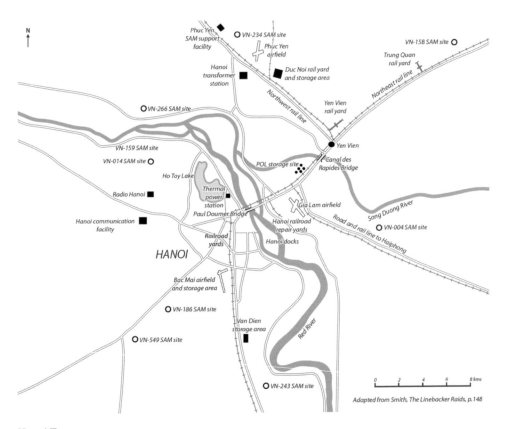

Hanoi Targets.

Above: Groundbreaking ECM technology incorporated into the EA-6A Prowler provided the Navy with a valuable tool for jamming North Vietnamese guidance and acquisition radars. (Photo U.S. Navy)

Below: Haiphong and its surrounding military and economic facilities found themselves under near continuous attack by Navy aircraft during the last half of December 1972. (Photo National Archives)

F-4s with one MiG-21 going down from fuel exhaustion after being relentlessly pursued. The first two B-52 strikes went off without a hitch, but the four cells attacking Bac Mai encountered heavy and accurate missile fire that downed two of the 307th SW bombers. Both crews abandoned their flaming aircraft; three crewmen went down with their plane and the remaining nine others were taken prisoner after bailing out.[53]

The loss of the second bomber also created an international incident when the bomb train from the stricken B-52 went astray, resulting in major damage to the nearby Bac Mai hospital and killing 28 staff members. The North Vietnamese were quick to capitalize on the incident as a clear example of "American carpet bombing" of the capital, when in fact planners went out of their way to limit collateral damage and civilian casualties.[54] It didn't help that a group of American anti-war activists were in Hanoi at the time and produced a number of highly exaggerated accounts about the indiscriminate bombing of the city that stoked the fires of outrage. The reality, however, was quite different. Large parts of Hanoi were completely untouched as the bombing was concentrated on specific areas. And despite the weight of more than 20,000 tons of bombs—on par with the most destructive raids of World War II—during the eleven-day campaign, the level of civilian casualties was remarkably low. Official North Vietnamese figures listed 1,318 dead in Hanoi and another 306 in Haiphong, a sharp contrast from the more than 40,000 German civilians who died during a nine-day and 10,000-ton bombing campaign against Hamburg in 1944.[55]

As a result of the Eighth Air Force's learning curve, the B-52 raids over the course of the next three days in the run-up to Christmas were markedly different in terms of target selection and modified operational tactics.

First, on December 22, F-111s launched nighttime strikes against ten targets in the Hanoi area, including airfields, radar and communication facilities, transshipment points, and port facilities. One F-111A of the 429th TFS out of Takhli was fatally hit by anti-aircraft fire during its attack on port facilities on the Red River; both crew ejected and were taken prisoner.[56] This time however the target for the B-52s was not Hanoi, but Haiphong and the 30-plane strike force out of U-Tapao flew inbound from the Gulf of the Tonkin. Navy A-6s preemptively struck nearly a dozen SAM sites and 16 F-4 chaff bombers created an enormous chaff cloud 30 miles long by 12 miles wide over the Haiphong area. Meanwhile, nearby Air Force EB-66s and offshore Navy Intruder and Skywarrior jammers took up their positions.[57] Eighteen B-52Ds hit the city's main POL storage facility and another 12 struck Haiphong's rail siding, creating massive secondary explosions and bellowing clouds of smoke. Only 43 SA-2s were fired with none scoring hits, highlighting the effectiveness of the Navy's suppression efforts and the ten Wild Weasel attacks on active site signals during the bombing.[58]

The next day tactical airstrikes against continued. Weather forced the cancellation of several F-4 laser-guided bombing missions against rail bridges north of Hanoi. Resorting to radar bombing and led by LORAN-equipped F-4s Pathfinders, 32 Phantoms armed with MK-82 500-pound conventional bombs struck Hanoi radio and communications facilities, while another 24 A-7Ds hit the Hoa Lac airfield with MK-82 bombs. To the east, Navy A-6s and A-7s pounded enemy air defenses, storage depots, railyards, power plants, and port facilities in and around Haiphong. Anti-aircraft gunners were busy, but few SA-2s were

Remnants of a military vehicle repair and storage facility following an Air Force tactical air strike in December 1972. (Photo National Archives)

Aerial reconnaissance photo showing damage to Bac Mai hospital when the bomb train from a stricken B-52 went astray on December 21, killing 28 hospital staff members and provoking international outrage. (Photo National Archives)

The worst accident of Linebacker II occurred on December 26 when a B-52 bomb train missed it target and destroyed a nearly mile-long stretch of Kham Thien street in Hanoi, resulting in the deaths of more than 200 civilians. (Photo National Archives)

fired at the attackers, as the missiles were apparently being saved for the B-52s raids. Like previous days, only a handful of MiG fighters rose to engage the strike or supporting aircraft, but none of these encounters resulted in the shooting downing of a plane by either side.

December 23 saw an even greater and unexpected shift in the night B-52 bombing effort. Catching the North Vietnamese defenders completely off guard, a 30-plane strike consisting of 18 B-52Ds from U-Tapao and 12 B-52Ds from Andersen flew within 18 miles of the Chinese border to unleash more than 800 tons of bombs on the Lang Dang railyard and pummel three nearby SAM sites.[59] In the meantime F-111s flew airfield suppression missions against the MiG bases at Kep, Phuc Yen, and Yen Bai. Only four or five SA-2s managed to be launched with none scoring hits, but four MiG-21s were able to engage and fire on two of the departing bomber cells with Atoll missiles. All missed.

On Christmas Eve, just hours before the planned 36-hour stand down of operations, 30 U-Tapao B-52Ds struck railyards and rail facilities about 40 miles north of Hanoi. Eighteen bombers targeted the Thai Nguyen rail complex again, while 12 others bombed the Kep railyard.[60] Only about 20 missiles were fired, but heavy anti-aircraft fire damaged one bomber. Several MiGs were also able to get airborne and engage the strike force, but again they failed to score any hits. One of the attacking MiG-21s, however, was shot down by a B-52, making this the second MiG kill of the campaign for the tail gunners.

All air operations over North Vietnam came to a halt on midnight December 24 as a goodwill gesture in observance of Christmas and as a badly needed rest for the exhausted Air Force and Navy air and ground crews. But there was little time for much holiday celebration as planners were putting the finishing touches on an all-out effort that was to begin in less than 48 hours. It was meant to be "the most ambitious to date."[61]

One Last Push

Tactical airstrikes resumed on December 26 with 32 Air Force A-7s and 16 LORAN-equipped F-4s targeting Hanoi's main electrical transformer station in a single strike that caused moderate damage to the facility and temporarily disrupted power to the city's power grid.[62] Resistance was light, only a few SA-2 launches and no fighters rose to challenge the attackers and all planes returned safely. Meanwhile over in Haiphong, strike aircraft from the *America, Enterprise, Ranger,* and *Saratoga* resumed their daily strikes against the city and its defenses.

Over the course of the next several days, the Americans would maintain this high operational tempo by conducting some 100 tactical strikes a day against Hanoi and Haiphong targets.[63] During this period the Air Force would lose two F-4Es to Atoll air-to-air missiles during aerial engagements with MiG-21s, the only U.S. fighter losses of Linebacker II.[64]

It was later on the night of December 26, however, that the Americans began delivering their aerial body blow by returning in force with 120 bombers—45 B-52Gs and 33 B-52Ds from Andersen and 42 B-52Ds from U-Tapao—to bomb ten targets in and around Hanoi and Haiphong.[65] Unlike the first days of the campaign, ten waves of bombers would now attack from seven different directions, at varying altitudes and spacing between cells, and exit from a different direction "in a single, simultaneous assault in order to overwhelm North Vietnam's air defenses."[66] The number of supporting Air Force aircraft had also grown to 75 that now included 23 F-4s to dispense large chaff clouds over the target areas,

By early January 1973 both the North Vietnamese and American delegations to the Paris peace talks came to the realization that a negotiated end to the war was within their grasp; a draft agreement was initialed on January 23 and the formal peace accords signed on January 27.

the addition of F-4E killer teams armed with cluster bombs, and 34 F-4 fighter flying strike escort and MiG combat air patrol.[67] This sizable support force was further augmented by nearly 40 more Navy aircraft flying Iron Hand, combat air patrol, and ECM missions. The latter included new Marine EA-6A Prowlers out of Da Nang that had the capability to effectively jam the modified Fire Can radars.[68]

Nothing was being left to chance and morale was high.

With F-111s just completing their bombing runs against the airfields at Kep, Hoa Lac, Phuc Yen, and Yen Bai, the ten waves of B-52s converged on their targets at 2230 amid heavy flak and SA-2s filling the skies. With time to resupply and reequip since the last strikes, the North Vietnamese defenders were ready. Colonel James McCarthy, the mission airborne commander in the lead aircraft of the 43rd SW, remarked later that "after 26 SAMs, I stopped counting" and "at bombs away, it looked like we were right in the middle of a fireworks factory that was in the process of blowing up."[69] Soon railroad yards, storage facilities, and POL depots in and around Hanoi were being rocked by the weight of bombs from 90 B-52s. It was in the midst of this chaos that a bomb train went astray to annihilate a nearly mile-long stretch of Kham Thien street and killed more than 200 civilians in the worst accident of the campaign. Meanwhile over in Haiphong, 30 more of the bombers laid waste to city's railyard and the main electrical transformer station.

A few MiGs did manage to react, but were quickly chased off by the F-4 escorts. Two B-52Ds from the 307th SW, however, were hit by SA-2s with the one, *Ebony 01*, becoming engulfed in flames following its bombing of the Giap Nhi railyard and then crashing southwest of Hanoi. The other, *Ash 01*, although badly damaged during an attack on the Kinh No rail complex, was able to make it to U-Tapao before crashing about a mile short of the runway. In all six crewmen were killed and four others were captured.[70]

The next night was to be a similar, yet smaller repeat with 36 B-52Ds from Andersen and U-Tapao striking Hanoi's railyards and storage depots, while 21 Guam-based B-52Gs with their unmodified ECM gear attacked the Lang Dang railyard near the Chinese border again.[71] In a new twist this time around, several SA-2 sites around Hanoi were also targeted by the big bombers as part of an intensified effort to destroy and not simply suppress the SAM sites. F-111s also hit a missile site for the first time in addition to their nighttime preemptive strikes against airfields. Likewise, earlier in the day Air Force Wild Weasels hunter-killer teams decimated several of Hanoi's SA-2 batteries with modified AGM-45s and cluster bombs, while Navy A-6 Iron Hands worked over air defense positions with 500-pound bombs and AGM-78 anti-radiation missiles to the east of the city.

Still the North Vietnamese defenders managed to launch some 70 missiles that night, which damaged one bomber and fatally crippled two others. One B-52D attached to the 43rd SW, *Cobalt 02*, had one of three missiles explode near it during its attack on the Trung Quang railyard northeast of Hanoi. The explosion killed one crewman outright, ruptured the fuel tanks, and set the plane alight. Four of the surviving crew members were captured and one was missing in action.[72] The other B-52D, *Ash 02*, with the 307th SW out of Guam was caught in a missile barrage while attacking a SAM site southwest of Hanoi and heavily damaged by shrapnel explosions. Amazingly, the pilot, Captain John Mize, was able to steering the burning and disabled aircraft into Thai air space before

The fighting ends.

having to abandon the plane near Nakhon Phanom. All the crew ejected and were rescued. For his heroics Captain Mize was awarded the Air Force Cross—the only Strategic Air Command member so honored during the war.[73]

The next two nights witnessed 60-plane bomber raids (with both Andersen and U-Tapao providing 30 B-52s each) on the North's main SA-2 missile storage and support facilities and multiple SAM sites, as well as against the now heavily bombed Lang Dang rail complex.[74] Increasingly F-111s targeted SAM sites near Hanoi at night, while Korat-based Wild Weasel hunter-killer teams pummeled the air defenses during the day. By December 28, 15 B-52s and 32 A-7Ds had inflicted heavy damage on the Trai Ca SAM support facility near Thai Nguyen, while the North's primary SAM storage facility at Phuc Yen had been completely destroyed by 45 B-52 sorties.[75]

The physical and psychological wear was beginning to show in the waning days of December as the North's defenses appeared to falter. Only about 20 missile launches were noted each night by the bomber crews now. Air Force Wild Weasels reported an increasingly lack of radar signals and tactical airstrikes noticed much lighter anti-aircraft fire than in the past. A few MiGs still rose to challenge the attackers, but dogfights on December 28 resulted in the downing of two MiG-21s in separate engagements by an Air Force F-4D from the 555th TFS and a Navy F-4J with VF-142 off the *Enterprise*.[76] As the final B-52 cell pulled away from its bombing run on the Trai Ca SAM support facility a few

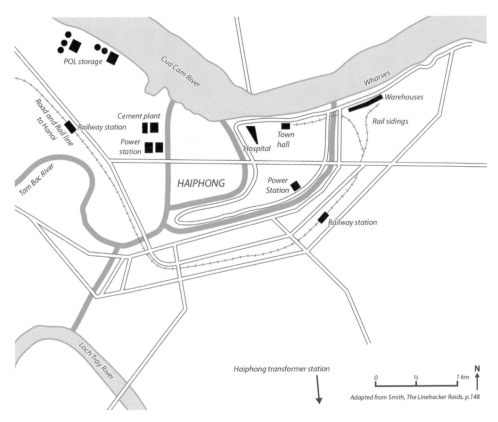

Haiphong Targets.

minutes before midnight on December 29, word was coming down from the Joint Chiefs that all air operations over North Vietnam north of the 20th parallel would cease by 0700 Hanoi time. Linebacker II was over. Hanoi had agreed to return to the peace talks in Paris.

The end of December's aerial assault on Hanoi and Haiphong did not bring an immediate end to the war or the end of bombing south of the 20th parallel, which would continue for almost another month. Peace would have to wait until the diplomats ironed out the final details of a settlement that was acceptable to the powers that be in Washington, Hanoi, and Saigon. Fortunately, the march of political and military events since the collapse of the proposed October agreement had convinced all concerned that now was the time for peace—even an imperfect and flawed one. Nixon's forceful military response to the Easter Offensive and his willingness to escalate the bombing campaign against the North had demonstrated American resolve, reassured its South Vietnamese ally, and set the stage for an honorable withdrawal that was internationally and domestically palatable. Le Duan and the politburo saw the wisdom of permanently removing the American military as a factor in their struggle with the South and the benefit of placating the wishes of their Soviet and Chinese patrons to de-escalate Cold War tensions. Hanoi also went to great lengths to portray Linebacker II as the "Dien Bien Phu in the skies" with

Former American POWs celebrate wheels-up and their freedom as Operation Homecoming gets underway in February 1973. (Photo Department of Defense)

wild exaggerations of American aircraft losses—34 B-52s and 47 other aircraft[77]—so as to counter any perception of North Vietnamese capitulation. For its part, the Thieu regime was caught in the middle and had little choice but to accept the agreement or face a complete cut-off of all future U.S. assistance and at least a ceasefire bought it some time.

Not surprisingly then, once peace talks between Kissinger and Le Tho resumed on January 8 swift progress was made. Outstanding differences were resolved or at least papered over. Side protocols on implementation were drawn up, secret understandings made or private assurances given on any remaining issues of contention, and timetables finalized. Kissinger and Tho initialed the agreement in Paris on January 23 with the formal signing by Secretary of State William Rogers taking place on January 27, 1973. America's active involvement in the Vietnam War was finally over.

7. POST-MORTEM

Over the course of the most intense six months of air operations in 1972 against the North—Operations Linebacker I & II—American pilots would fly almost 44,000 combat sorties and drop 175,918 tons of bombs.[1] It was, however, those eleven days in late December that would produce the most iconic images of massive B-52 bomber unleashing 15,237 tons of bombs on 34 targets across the North Vietnamese heartland.[2] The North responded as best it could with MiG fighters, intensive anti-aircraft barrages, and by launching between 800 and 1,200 SA-2 missiles.[3] At day's end, the 1972 campaign would cost the United States 107 aircraft—including 15 B-52s—and the lives of 93 pilots and crew to hostile fire; the VPAF lost 68 fighter aircraft in return.[4]

While this would be the final act of America's eight-year, on-again-off-again air war against North Vietnam, it would set the stage for a debate over the role and effectiveness of the bombing—and particularly of Linebacker II—in ending the war and in the broader historical context of the utility of using air power to advance political objectives.

Certainly the 1972 air campaign inflicted substantial damage to the North Vietnamese economic and military infrastructure and hindered Hanoi's war-making capability. The ongoing destruction of bridges, rail links, truck repair and storage facilities, and transshipment points diverted extensive manpower and material resources into repairing and maintaining some semblance of the country's transportation and logistics network. By the late summer the flow of supplies southward had been sharply reduced and it was believed that less than 20 percent of previous supplies were actually reaching frontline North Vietnamese units.[5] Industrial production likewise suffered as a result of repeated airstrikes and large quantities of war matériel and supplies went up in smoke under the weight of American bombing. Linebacker II alone was credited with damaging or destroying 1,600 military complexes, 372 rail cars, 25 percent of POL stockpiles, and 80 percent of the North's electrical power production.[6] In addition, the once-vaunted North Vietnamese air defenses were shattered by the end of December; surface-to-air missile inventories had been largely exhausted or destroyed and the once potent MiG fighter threat largely neutralized, leaving the North as exposed and vulnerable as ever.

There can also be little doubt that overwhelming American and South Vietnamese air power was a decisive factor in smashing the North Vietnamese Easter Offensive and eviscerating Hanoi's attempt to achieve a conclusive military victory over the Saigon government in 1972. Moreover, Hanoi was clearly caught off guard by the American response and Nixon's willingness to escalate at a time when the United States was militarily disengaging from Southeast Asia. Thus, for the second time in four years Le Duan was forced to adopt a longer-term political strategy to defeat the Thieu government and its American ally.

In contrast, the Nixon White House was forced to rely on its last remaining form of military leverage in Vietnam, air power, to achieve its political objective of a negotiated peace settlement. Starting with Freedom Train and its evolution into Linebacker I, the escalating

Table: U.S. Aircraft Losses, Linebacker II, December 18-28, 1972

DATE	TYPE	CALL SIGN	TARGET	CAUSE
18th	F-111A	Snug 40	Hanoi Radio	Unknown
18th	B-52G	Charcoal 01	Yen Vien Complex	SA-2
18th	B-52G	Peach 02	Yen Vien Complex	SA-2
18th	A-7C	Streetcar 303	(Iron Hand)	SA-2
18th	B-52D	Rose 01	Hanoi Radio	SA-2
20th	B-52D	Quilt 03	Yen Vien Complex	SA-2
20th	B-52G	Brass 02	Yen Vien Complex	SA-2
20th	B-52G	Orange 03	Yen Vien Complex	SA-2
20th	A-6A	Milestone 511	Haiphong Shipyard	SA-2
20th	B-52D	Straw 02	Gia Lam Railyard	SA-2
20th	B-52G	Olive 01	Kinh No Rail Complex	SA-2
20th	B-52G	Tan 03	Kinh No Rail Complex	SA-2
21st	A-6A	Flying Ace 500	Kien An Airfield	AAA
21st	B-52D	Scarlet 03	Bac Mai Airfield Complex	SA-2
21st	B-52D	Blue 01	Bac Mai Airfield Complex	SA-2
22nd	F-111A	Jackle 33	Hanoi Port Facility	Unknown
23rd	EB-66	Hunt 02	(Non-combat loss)	Engine failure
23rd	F-4J		(Photo escort)	AAA
24th	A-7E	Battle Cry 314	(Mine laying)	Suspected AAA
26th	B-52D	Ebony 02	Giap Nhi Railyard	SA-2
26th	B-52D	Ash 01	Kinh No Rail Complex	SA-2
27th	F-4E	DeSoto 03	(Strike escort)	MiG-21
27th	F-4E	Vega 02	(Combat air patrol)	MiG-21
27th	HH-52	Jolly Green	(Rescue)	Small arms
27th	B-52D	Ash 02	SW Hanoi SAM site	SA-2
27th	B-52D	Cobalt 02	Truang Quang Railyard	SA-2
28th	RA-5C	Flint River 603	(Photo recon)	MiG-21

Sources: Project CHECO, "Linebacker Operations, September-December 1972," Appendix 5, p. 95; C. Hobson, *Vietnam Air Losses*, pp. 242-246.

American bombing campaign against the North was driven by the need to interdict the flow of men and matériel southward. Although past interdiction efforts had come up short, the Americans had little choice; it was either that or face the collapse of the Saigon government. The largely successful effort this time, for it surely stymied Hanoi's efforts to resupply and reequip its forces in the South, was a result of the enormous amount of American air assets committed, the willingness to mine North Vietnamese ports, and the conventional nature of the North's military in 1972. Air power proved to be the right tool at the right time.

Time, however, was working against both the Americans and North Vietnamese and it would ultimately drive Washington and Hanoi toward a compromise. Nixon needed to get out of Vietnam. Despite his recent reelection, Nixon's room for maneuver was quickly evaporating as congressional pressure was mounting and the final withdrawal of U.S. troops was underway in early 1973. Le Duan needed the Americans out of Vietnam. Given time to rebuild and reequip, the North was confident of victory over the Saigon government once the weight of American support was removed. Likewise, Hanoi was under growing pressure from its key allies, Moscow and Beijing, to reach a peace agreement as Washington's policy of détente and rapprochement began to bear fruit. All that was now needed was a final catalyst for action.

Linebacker II prove to be that catalyst by serving notice that the Americans were willing to inflict even more military, economic, and psychological pain on the North Vietnamese to achieve a politically acceptable settlement. Since Hanoi was getting most of what it wanted, i.e., troops remaining in the South and control over territory it occupied there, it was not worth the risk of calling Washington's hand. Importantly too, President Thieu got an unequivocal message of current American military support and assurances of future treaty enforcement should Hanoi violate the ceasefire. This proved to be enough to overcome the last remaining obstacles to peace and within weeks Kissinger and Tho were able to finalize a peace agreement that both sides could claim as a victory.

The use of air power this time made a difference both militarily and politically, largely because of timing and the confluence of events that made the war ripe for a peace settlement at the end of 1972. Conditions that were not in existence a year earlier let alone in 1968 when both sides were seeking to overcome adversity and still held out hope of victory on the battlefield. Neither side got all they wanted, but each got just enough. To their credit Washington and Hanoi realized this time there was a window of opportunity for peace and seized it. This was the final tribute to the warriors of the 1972 air war.

NOTES

1. Searching for Peace with Honor

1. D. Schmitz, *Richard Nixon and the Vietnam War*, p. 46.
2. "National Security Advisor Memorandum for the President," March 16, 1969. As cited in Schmitz, p. 48.
3. Richard Nixon, "Vietnamization Speech," November 3, 1969.
4. D. Fulghum and Maitland, *South Vietnam on Trial*, p. 52.
5. Schmitz, p. 68.
6. Ibid., p. 82.
7. Ibid., p. 82.
8. R. Nixon, *No More Vietnams*, p. 141.
9. Schmitz, p. 84.
10. Ibid., p. 88.
11. Ibid., p. 120.
12. Nixon, p. 137-138.
13. Schmitz, p. 121.
14. W. Isaacson, *Kissinger*, p. 244.
15. Schmitz, p. 135.

2. The Year of the Rat—A Time of Decision

1. W. Isaacson, *Kissinger*, p. 398.
2. J. Morrocco, *Rain of Fire*, p. 96.
3. E. Hartsook and S. Slade, *Air War Vietnam*, p. 179.
4. C. Hobson, *Vietnam Air Losses*, pp. 211-217.
5. Hartsook and Slade, p. 224.
6. Ibid., p. 132.
7. Ibid., pp. 131-133.
8. Ibid., p. 224.
9. Ibid., pp. 172-173.
10. Ibid., p. 178.
11. Morrocco, p. 100.
12. L. Nguyen, *Hanoi's War*, p. 228.
13. P. Asselin, *A Bitter Peace*, p. 38.
14. Hartsook and Slade, pp. 175.
15. Ibid., p. 176.
16. Ibid., p. 177
17. Morrocco, p. 101.
18. Hobson, p. 217.
19. Hartsook and Slade, p.260.
20. Hobson, p. 218.
21. D. Fulghum and Maitland, *South Vietnam on Trial*, p. 138.
22. Morrocco, pp. 106-107.
23. D. Middleton, *Air War – Vietnam*, p. 201.
24. Ibid., p. 107.
25. Hartsook and Slade, p. 273.

26. Ibid., p. 303.
27. Ibid., p. 308.
28. Hobson, pp. 220-226.

3. American Air Power Heads North

1. J. Smith, *The Linebacker Raids*, p. 51.
2. W. Isaacson, *Kissinger*, p. 417.
3. E. Hartsook and S. Slade, *Air War Vietnam*, p. 221.
4. R. Francillon, *Tonkin Gulf Yacht Club*, pp. 126, 131, 135.
5. J. Morrocco, *Rain of Fire*, p. 102.
6. C. Hobson, *Vietnam Air Losses*, pp. 266, 253.
7. Morrocco, p. 109; Hartsook and Slade, pp. 290-291; D. Middleton, *Air War – Vietnam*, p. 125.
8. Morrocco, p. 108.
9. Smith, p. 57.
10. Hartsook and Slade, p. 284.
11. Ibid., p. 285.
12. W. Thompson, *To Hanoi and Back*, p. 227.
13. W. Boyne, "Breaking the Dragon's Jaw," *Air Force Magazine*, p. 60; Thompson, p. 235.
14. D. McCarthy, *MiG Killers*, pp. 108-109.
15. Smith, p. 58.
16. Hobson, pp. 221-223.
17. K. Eschmann, *Linebacker*, p. 12.
18. Ibid., p. 13.
19. Morrocco, pp. 109-110.
20. Ibid., p. 110.
21. Thompson, p. 226.
22. Morrocco, p. 110.
23. Hobson, p. 222.
24. Eschmann, pp. 15-16.
25. Morrocco, p. 110.
26. Ibid., p. 131.
27. Hartsook and Slade, p. 295.
28. Morrocco, p. 130.
29. Ibid., p. 131.
30. N. Brizer and P. Mersky, *Navy A-7 Corsair II Units*, p. 44.
31. J. Ethell, *One Day in a Long War*, pp. 32-34.
32. Ibid., p. 46.
33. Ibid., pp. 50-51.
34. S. Emerson, *Air War Over North Vietnam*, p. 94; Morrocco, p. 131; Ethell, p. 50.
35. Ethell, p. 50.
36. Hobson, p. 224.
37. Thompson, pp. 35-36.
38. Ethell, p. 50.
39. Hobson, p. 225.
40. Ethell, p. 131.
41. Smith, p. 73; Hobson pp. 224-225.
42. Middleton, p. 252.
43. Smith, p. 76; G. Hartmann and S. Truver, "Weapons that Wait," p. 152.
44. Morrocco, p. 136.
45. Ibid., p. 136.

46. Hartsook and Slade, p. 298.
47. Hobson, pp. 224-227.

4. Turning the Tide

1. S. Emerson, *Air War Over North Vietnam*, p. 48.
2. W. Thompson, *To Hanoi and Back*, pp. 242-243.
3. M. Michel, *The 11 Days of Christmas*, pp. 49-50, 89.
4. Thompson, p. 244; D. Middleton, *Air War – Vietnam*, p. 258.
5. J. Nichols and B. Tillman, *On Yankee Station*, p. 56.
6. Ibid.
7. Ibid, pp. 56-57.
8. K. Eschmann, *Linebacker*, p. 42.
9. Ibid., p. 26.
10. C. Hobson, *Vietnam Air Losses*, pp. 225-226.
11. J. Morrocco, *Rain of Fire*, p. 141.
12. I. Toperczer, *MiG-17 and MiG-19 Units*, p. 58
13. Thompson, p. 242.
14. Ibid., p. 237.
15. Eschmann, pp. 30-31.
16. J. Smith, *The Linebacker Raids*, p. 86.
17. Morrocco, p. 130.
18. E. Hartsook and S. Slade, *Air War Vietnam Plans and Operations*, p. 298.
19. Project CHECO Report, "Linebacker: Overview of the First 120 Days," p. 25.
20. Smith, p. 84.
21. Morrocco, p. 136.
22. Ibid.
23. Thompson, p. 248.
24. Ibid.
25. Hartsook and Slade, p. 299; Smith, p. 83.
26. Hartsook and Slade, p. 301.
27. Smith, p. 84; Morrocco, p. 138.
28. "Evaluation of Guided Bomb Systems Employed in SEA," Institute of Defense Analysis, Arlington, VA, May 1974, pp. 39-41.
29. M. Mitchel, *Clashes*, p. 240.
30. Hobson, pp. 224-230.
31. Morrocco, p. 144.
32. R. Boniface, *MiGs Over North Vietnam*, p. 100.
33. Hobson, p. 271; D. McCarthy, *MiG Killers*, p. 156.
34. Thompson, pp. 238-239.
35. Mitchel, pp. 258-259.
36. Thompson, p. 240.
37. Ibid.
38. McCarthy, pp. 155-157.
39. Morrocco, p. 145.
40. Nichols and Tillman, p. 114.
41. Hobson, pp. 224-233.
42. Mitchel, p. 258.
43. Morrocco, p. 140.
44. Hobson, p. 271.
45. Hartsook and Slade, p. 305.

46. Ibid., p. 312.
47. Ibid., p. 318.
48. D. Fulghum and T. Maitland, *South Vietnam on Trial*, pp. 183-184.
49. Ibid., p. 183.
50. P. Asselin, *A Bitter Peace*, pp. 60-62.

5. The Illusion of Peace

1. J. Morrocco, *Rain of Fire*, p. 136.
2. J. Smith, *The Linebacker Raids*, p. 98.
3. Ibid.
4. M. Mitchell, *Clashes*, p. 250.
5. Smith, p. 103.
6. C. Hobson, *Vietnam Air Losses*, p. 235.
7. R. Francillon, *Tokin Gulf Yacht Club*, pp. 118-161.
8. Hobson, pp. 235-238.
9. S. Emerson, *Air War Over North Vietnam*, p. 113.
10. Hobson, p. 237.
11. W. Thompson, *To Hanoi and Back*, p. 246.
12. Hobson, p. 237; Smith, p. 108.
13. Thompson, p. 246.
14. Smith, p. 183.
15. McCarthy, *MiG Killers*, pp. 156-15; Hobson, p. 238.
16. Smith, p. 115; Thompson, p. 242.
17. Hobson, p. 231.
18. Smith, p. 110; R. Boniface, *MiGs Over North Vietnam*, p. 118.
19. Hobson, *Table: US Fixed-Wing Losses to Surface-to-Air Missiles*, p. 271
20. Smith, p. 110.
21. Ibid., p. 112.
22. P. Asselin, *A Bitter Peace*, p. 77.
23. Ibid., p. 76.
24. W. Isaacson, *Kissinger*, pp. 447-448.
25. Asselin, p. 80.
26. Isaacson, p. 448
27. Smith, p. 114.
28. Ibid., p. 115.
29. Ibid., p. 115.
30. Nguyen, *Hanoi's War*, p. 280.
31. Ibid., pp. 280-281.
32. Asselin, p. 92; E. Hartsook and S. Slade, *Air War Vietnam Plans and Operations*, p. 323.
33. Hartsook and Slade, p. 322.
34. Asselin, pp. 93-94.
35. Ibid., p. 94.
36. Ibid., p. 95.
37. Nguyen, p. 285.

6. Unleashing the Dogs of War

1. Nguyen, p. 290.
2. Ibid., p. 291.
3. P. Asselin, *A Bitter Peace*, p. 119.
4. Ibid., p. 144.

5. W. Thompson, *To Hanoi and Back*, p. 258.
6. E. Hartsook and S. Slade, *Air War Vietnam Plans and Operations*, p. 270.
7. Thompson, p. 224.
8. K. Eschmann, *Linebacker*, p. 77.
9. J. Smith, *The Linebacker Raids*, p. 121.
10. The original Operation Linebacker that began on May 10 and was still continuing south of the 20th parallel was now officially renamed Linebacker I to distinguish it from the new bombing campaign planned for north of the 20th parallel.
11. Eschmann, p. 75.
12. Ibid., p. 75.
13. Eschmann, p. 77; R. Francillon, *Tonkin Gulf Yacht Club*, pp. 117-161.
14. Eschmann, p. 77.
15. Ibid., p. 79.
16. C. Hobson, *Vietnam Air Losses*, pp. 243-245.
17. Eschmann, p. 74.
18. Ibid.
19. Ibid.
20. J. Morrocco, *Rain of Fire*, p. 146.
21. Eschmann, p. 91.
22. J. McCarthy and G. Allison, *Linebacker II*, p. 42.
23. Morrocco, p. 149.
24. Ibid., p. 149.
25. Morrocco, p. 149; Hobson, p. 242.
26. Morrocco, p. 150; Smith, p. 129.
27. Eschmann, p. 104.
28. Hobson, p. 242.
29. Eschmann, p. 107.
30. Hobson, p. 242.
31. Hartsook and Slade, p. 333.
32. Eschmann, p. 111.
33. Ibid., pp. 139-140.
34. J. Sherwood, "Nixon's Trident," p. 71.
35. Hobson, pp. 242-243.
36. Gonzales, "The Mining Campaigns of Vietnam," p. 4.
37. Hobson, p. 245.
38. Eschmann, pp. 112-114.
39. Ibid., pp. 114-115.
40. McCarthy and Allison, p. 80.
41. Eschmann, p. 116.
42. Ibid.
43. Hobson, pp. 242-243.
44. Eschmann, pp. 131-133.
45. Hobson, p. 243.
46. Eschmann, p. 134; Morrocco, p. 150.
47. Eschmann, p. 134.
48. Asselin, p. 150.
49. Morrocco, p. 152.
50. Despite some conflicting accounts and interpretations, Brigadier General James McCarthy (ret.), who was then commanding the 43rd SW on Guam, clearly states that "the weight of the effort for Day Four had already been established as coming from the D fleet at U-Tapao, independent of the previous day's results." McCarthy and Allison, p. 91.

51. Eschmann, p. 137.
52. Ibid., p. 140.
53. Hobson, p. 244.
54. Eschmann, p. 147.
55. Morrocco, p. 160.
56. Hobson, p. 244.
57. Eschmann, p. 154.
58. McCarthy and Allison, p. 100; Eschmann, p. 155.
59. Eschmann, p. 156.
60. Ibid., p. 159.
61. McCarthy and Allison, p. 121.
62. Eschmann, p. 163.
63. Project CHECO, "Linebacker Operations," Appendix 6, pp. 100-101.
64. Hobson, pp. 245-246.
65. Eschmann, p. 163.
66. Morrocco, p. 154.
67. Project CHECO, Appendix 7, p. 103.
68. Eschmann, p. 150.
69. Morrocco, p. 156.
70. Hobson, p. 245.
71. Eschmann, p. 183.
72. Hobson, p. 246.
73. Ibid.
74. Eschmann, p. 183, pp. 190-191.
75. Ibid., p. 192.
76. D. McCarthy, *MiG Killers*, p. 157.
77. Asselin, p. 152.

7. Post-Mortem

1. M. Clodfelter, *Vietnam in Military Statistics*, p. 224; W. Head, "Linebacker Operations and the U.S. Strategic Bombing," p. 20.
2. Head, p. 20.
3. See M. Michel, *The 11 Day of Christmas*, for an interesting discussion about the number of SAMs actually fired during Linebacker II, pp. 248-249.
4. C. Hobson, *Vietnam Air Losses*, pp. 224-241; Project CHECO, "Linebacker Operations" Appendix C, pp. 71-72; E. Hartsook and S. Slade, *Air War Vietnam Plans and Operations*, p. 339.
5. K. Eschmann, *Linebacker*, p. 57.
6. J. Morrocco, *Rain of Fire*, p. 157.

BIBLIOGRAPHY

Asselin, Pierre. *A Bitter Peace: Washington, Hanoi, and the Making of the Paris Agreement.* Chapel Hill, NC: University of North Carolina Press, 2002.

Boniface, Roger. *MiGs over North Vietnam: The Vietnam People's Air Force in Combat, 1965–75.* Mechanicsburg, PA: Stackpole Books, 2010.

Blackwelder, Donald. "The Long Road to Desert Storm and Beyond: The Development of Precision Guided Bombs." Air University, Maxwell Air Force Base, Alabama, 1992.

Boyne, Walter. "Linebacker II." *Air Force Magazine*, November 1997.

_____. "Breaking the Dragon's Jaw." *Air Force Magazine*, August 2011.

Brizer, Norman and Peter Mersky. *U.S. Navy A-7 Corsair II Units of the Vietnam War.* Oxford, UK: Osprey Publishing, 2004.

Clodfelter, Michael. *Vietnam in Military Statistics: A History of the Indochina Wars, 1772–1991.* Jefferson, NC: McFarland Publishing, 1995.

Correll, John. "The Emergence of Smart Bombs." *Air Force Magazine*, March 2010.

Department of the Navy. "Command History for 1972: VA-25." September 4, 1973.

Eschmann, Karl. *Linebacker: The Untold Story of the Air Raids over North Vietnam.* New York: Ivy Books, 1989.

Ethell, Jeffery and Alfred Price. *One Day in a Long War: May 10, 1972. Air War, North Vietnam.* New York: Random House, 1989.

Francillon, René. *Tonkin Gulf Yacht Club: U.S. Carrier Operations off Vietnam.* London: Conway Maritime Press Ltd, 1988. Naval Institute Press edition, Annapolis, MD.

Fulghum, David and Terrence Maitland. *The Vietnam Experience: South Vietnam on Trial, Mid-1970 to 1972.* Boston: Boston Publishing Company, 1984.

Gonzalez, Michael. "The Forgotten History: The Mining Campaigns of Vietnam, 1967–1973." War Stories Collection, Angelo State University, Texas, no date.

Greer, W. L.. "The 1972 Mining of Haiphong Harbor: A Case Study in Naval Mining and Diplomacy." Institute for Defense Analyses. April 1997.

Hartmann, Gregory and Scott Truver. *Weapons that Wait: Mine Warfare in the U.S. Navy.* Annapolis, MD: Naval Institute Press, 1991.

Hartsook, Elizabeth and Stuart Slade. *Air War: Vietnam Plans and Operations, 1969–1975.* Newtown, CT: Defense Lion Publications, 2012.

Head, William. "Linebacker Operations and U.S. Strategic Bombing at the End of the Second Indochina War." *Virginia Review of Asian Studies*, Summer 2006.

Headquarters PACAF, "Summary Air Operations Southeast Asia." April 1972.

Hobson, Chris. *Vietnam Air Losses. United States Air Force, Navy and Marine Corps Fixed-Wing Aircraft Losses in Southeast Asia 1961–1975.* Hinckley, UK: Midland Publishing, 2001.

Isaacson, Walter. *Kissinger: A Biography.* New York: Simon & Schuster, 1992.

Mailes, Yancy. "B-52s Played a Major Role in Operation Linebacker II." December 18, 2017.

Found at: www.andersen.af.mil/News/Features/Article/1398659/b-52-played-major-role-in-operation-linebacker-ii/

McCarthy, Donald. *MiG Killers: A Chronology of U.S. Air Victories in Vietnam 1965–1973.* North Branch, MN: Specialty Press, 2009.

McCarthy, James and George Allison. *Linebacker II: A View from the Rock.* Washington, DC: Office of Air Force History, Department of the Air Force, 1985.

Mersky, Peter and Norman Polmar. *The Naval Air War in Vietnam.* Annapolis, MD: The Nautical and Aviation Publishing Company of America, 1982.

Meyer, Jeffery. "Andersen AFB's Legacy: Operation Linebacker II." December 18, 2017. Found at www.andersen.af.mil/News/Commentaries/Display/Article/416815/andersen-afbs-legacy-operation-linebacker-ii/

Michel, Marshall. *Clashes: Air Combat over North Vietnam, 1965–1972.* Annapolis, MD: Naval Institute Press, 1997.

Michel, Marshall. *The 11 Days of Christmas: America's Last Vietnam Battle.* San Francisco, CA: Encounter Books, 2002.

Middleton, Drew. *Air War – Vietnam.* New York: Arno Press, 1978.

Morgan, Rick. *A-6 Intruder Units of the Vietnam War.* Oxford, UK: Osprey Publishing, 2012.

Morrocco, John. *The Vietnam Experience: Rain of Fire, Air War 1969–1973.* Boston: Boston Publishing Company, 1985.

The New York Times. "Text of U.S. Communique Listing Targets of Raids in North Vietnam," December 28, 1972.

Nguyen, Lien-Hang. *Hanoi's War: An International History of the War for Peace in Vietnam.* Chapel Hill, NC: University of North Carolina Press, 2012.

Nichols, John and Barrett Tillman. *On Yankee Station: The Naval Air War over Vietnam.* Annapolis, MD: Naval Institute Press, 1987.

Nixon, Richard. "Vietnamization Speech." November 3, 1969.

_____. *No More Vietnams.* New York: Arbor House, 1985.

Olsen, James. *In Country: The Illustrated Encyclopedia of the Vietnam War.* New York: Metro Books, 2008.

Project CHECO Southeast Asia Report. "Linebacker: Overview of the First 120 Days." September 27, 1973.

_____. "Linebacker Operations, September–December 1972." December 31, 1978.

Schmitz, David. *Richard Nixon and the Vietnam War.* Lanham, MD: Rowman & Littlefield, 2016.

Sherwood, John. "Nixon's Trident: Naval Power in Southeast Asia, 1968-1972." Washington, DC: Naval History & Heritage Command, Department of the Navy, 2009.

Smith, John. *The Linebacker Raids: The Bombing of North Vietnam, 1972.* London: Arms & Armour Press, 1998.

Thompson, Wayne. *To Hanoi and Back: The U.S. Air Force and North Vietnam, 1966-1973.* Washington, DC: Smithsonian Institute Press, 2000.

Topercza, Istvan. *MiG-17 and MiG-19 Units of the Vietnam War.* Oxford, UK: Osprey Publishing, 2001.

Index